Look Before You Leap

Steps to Your Child's Greatest
Success in Dance.

Pulling Back the Curtain
on the Dance Industry.

Dianne Leathem

Look Before You Leap
Steps to Your Child's Greatest Success in Dance.
Pulling Back the Curtain on the Dance Industry

First published in Australia by Dianne Leathem 2020
https://www.dancesuccess.org/

Copyright © Dianne Leathem 2020
All Rights Reserved

 A catalogue record for this book is available from the National Library of Australia

ISBN: 978-0-6489492-0-6 (pbk)
ISBN: 978-0-6489492-1-3 (ebk)

Typesetting and design by Publicious Book Publishing
Published in collaboration with Publicious Book Publishing
www.publicious.com.au

No part of this book may be reproduced in any form, by photocopying or by any electronic or mechanical means, including information storage or retrieval systems, without permission in writing from both the copyright owner and the publisher of this book.

Photograph credits:
Cover. Shuttershock_ 168086345 and Smile Click
1. Shutterstock_167062726
2. David-hofman_LpqYFDwr7io-unsplash
3. Ferdinand-studio-cmzc3OdZfsl-unsplash
4. Rosalie O'Connor
5. Shutterstock_167062726
6. Shutterstock_149414094
7. Dancers going onstage 1c7E73E2-8E9E
8. 41D045oc-ABCA-
9. Shuttershock
10. Lion Wolfe Photography
11. Major L Tonkin
12. Major L Tonkin
13. Smile Click

Dedication

This book is dedicated with gratitude to:

My dear mum and dad for giving me the gift of learning to dance;

All the teachers and mentors who have been such a special and inspiring part of my dance journey, including David Peake, Gillian Francis, Julia Barry, Lorraine Peters, Russell Kerr, Ann Judson, Robert Young, and Averil Binzer; and

My very dear friend, the late Beverly Millar, who loved ballet and dance as much as I do.

Preface

The following excerpts from the book *First Steps* by Ruth French and Felix Demery are words of wisdom that apply just as much today as when they were written in 1934:

> 'Dancing, combining as it does the complete use of the arms, head, body and legs, with artistry, feeling and expression, needs the full use of the mind as well as muscles.'

> 'Do not be in a hurry; remember that the Elementary is really the foundation of all the rest of the work. Make sure that that foundation is strong and lasting before attempting your Examination. Try to develop the artistic side, and to get feeling and expression into your dancing, realizing that all the exercises, etc., are only a means to an end. They are as necessary to the dancer as the notes and scales to the musician. The musician has one great advantage over the dancer – he can buy his instrument all ready to be played on, whereas to the dancer his body is his instrument and has to be built and tuned with care before he can express himself. Whether you are taking up dancing for health, pleasure, or as a future career it is all important that the foundational work be correct. The Syllabi of which we have been writing are the outcome of generations of work and thought, and should, if correctly taught and practised, do much to build a healthy, well-poised and equally-developed body, an alert and intelligent mind, perfectly controlled muscles, and that "joie de vivre" that comes from mental and physical fitness.'

> (published in Great Britain by A. Brown & Sons, Limited, Hull 1934. Revised in 1936, pp. v, 60)

Contents

Dedication iii

Preface v

Introduction: Pulling Back the Curtain
on the Dance Industry 1

Chapter 1: Problem One – Anyone Can Open a Dance
Studio and Teach Dancing 9
    Look before You Leap—or Gamble
    on a Blind Leap of Faith? 11
    The Parent–Teacher Tug of War 14
    Quality, Not Quantity 14

Chapter 2: Problem Two – The Alarming Rise in Injuries
Among Dance Students 17
    Stop Chasing the 'WOW' Factor 19
    The Worldwide Epidemic of Dangerous Stretching
    and Overtraining 21
    Warming Up is Not Stretching 25
        Purpose of warming up 25
        Cooling down 26
    What is Stretching, Overstretching and Extreme Stretching? 27
    Knowing the Different Types of Stretching 29
        Ballistic stretch 29
        Dynamic stretch 29
        Static stretch 30
        Prolonged stretch 30
        Proprioceptive Neuromuscular Facilitation (PNF) 30
        Overstretching and extreme stretching 30
    Dance is Art—Tricks Are Tricks 31

Chapter 3: Problem Three – The Global Sexualisation of Young Dance Students 33
    Age-Inappropriate Choreography 34

Chapter 4: Problem Four – Unqualified, Inexperienced Teachers 39

Chapter 5: Problem Five – Damaging Influences 41

Chapter 6: Other Problems in the Booming Dance Industry 44
    Not Everyone Can Be a Professional Dancer 45
    Power and Profits 46
    Big Fish in Little Ponds 48

Chapter 7: What is the Solution to These Problems? 49
    Duty of Care 50
    Parents Must Be Proactive 51
    Too Much of a Good Thing 52

Chapter 8: How to Choose the Best Dance Studio and Teacher for Your Child 53
    The Many Great Benefits of Learning to Dance 54
    The Importance of Technique 55
    Learning a Nationally or Internationally Recognised Syllabus in Each Style of Dance 55
    Looking for a Dance Studio 56
        Internet searches 56
        Beware the spin doctors 57
        Substance or spin 57
        Google reviews 59
        Word of mouth 59
        So what should you do? 60
    Types of Dance Studios 60
        Boutique studios 61
        'Hamburger with the lot' studios 63
    The Studio Floor 65
    Sound Levels in Dance Studios, at Workshops and Conventions 67
    Your Child's Digital Image 67

How to Avoid Having the Wool Pulled Over Your Eyes 68
    Buzzwords and advertising hooks 68
    'Family' as an advertising hook 69
    Beware too much praise 69
Your Checklist for Interviewing Prospective
Studios and Teachers 72
Mud Map of How Your Child's Classes Can Ideally Progress 74
Fees 74

Chapter 9: Starting Dance Classes 76

What Parents Should Ask Themselves 76
    What results do I expect to receive for my child through
    dancing lessons? 76
    At what age should my child start dance classes? 76
    Who will be teaching my child? 78
    What style/genre of dance is best for my child? 82
    How many hours a week should my child spend
    at dancing lessons? 87
Danger of Learning Too Many Styles Too Soon 89
Manners and Behaviour 90
    A word from the late Robert Young 92

Chapter 10: Competitions and Eisteddfods 94

The 'Art' of Dance is Being Sacrificed 96
Three Types of Dance Competition 98
    Traditional eisteddfod 98
    Competition franchises 99
    International competitions 99
Private/Individual Lessons 99

Chapter 11: Overtraining, Stress and Burnout 101

The Misuse and Overuse of the Term 'Elite' 102
The Misuse and Overuse of the Term 'Master Teacher' 104
What's the Rush? 104

Chapter 12: Full-time Training 106

Some Concerns to Note 106
Some Advice for Students Considering Full-Time Training 107
    Why do you want to do this? 107

    Who should pursue full-time training? 110
    What should you train in? 111
    How are you going to pay for the course? 112
    When should you start full-time training? 112

Chapter 13: Dance Jobs and Career Prospects 114

Chapter 14: Home-schooling 119

Chapter 15: Summer Programs 121

Chapter 16: Examinations 124
    What Are the Benefits of Sitting Exams for Dance? 125

Chapter 17: Concerts 127

Chapter 18: Bullying 130

Chapter 19: Body Image, Nutrition and Overall Care 132

**Chapter 20: Dance Attire, Shoes, Costumes,
Hair and Makeup 134**

Chapter 21: Code of Conduct for Parents 139
    Parents Must Not Try to Run the Dance Studio 140

Chapter 22: What Dance Professionals Say 143
    Nicole Ashfield – Dip ABS, LATOD, ARAD 143
    Paul Malek 150
    Gina-Marie Leathem ARAD Solo Seal 158

Chapter 23: Conclusion 162

For more information 164
    Useful Websites 164
    Recognised Dance Syllabus Organisations 164
    Resources Available at https://www.dancesuccess.org 165

About the Author 166

INTRODUCTION

Pulling Back the Curtain on the Dance Industry

Guiding your child to their greatest success in dance relies on your vigilant research to gain accurate knowledge and information. Whether your child learns dancing as a recreational hobby or hopes to become a professional dancer, here you will find the steps that will help you guide your child on a successful, happy and safe dance journey.

You child may be on the pathway to success—or just on the goat track out to the back paddock!

You may think your child is already receiving the best, and the safest, dance training—but, armed with greater knowledge, you may need to think again.

The Upside and the Downside

Dance is an absolutely wonderful hobby for children of all ages. On the upside, they can gain enjoyment moving to music, improve fitness, make friends, experience performing onstage, and many other benefits. Parents who send their children to dance lessons must be applauded for giving them the gift of dance. They do so in good faith and trust in the studio owners and teachers. However, there is a downside. Dance training can be astonishingly damaging.

It has never been more important for parents to become as informed as they possibly can to avoid this damage.

How you guide your children in dance can make or break them.

You will be shocked to know that hidden behind an attractively alluring curtain is a world-wide epidemic of overstretching, overtraining, dangerous teaching methods, and unqualified, inexperienced teachers. This epidemic, together with the global sexualisation of young dancers, is causing damage to dance students.

It's time to shine the spotlight on the problems in today's world of dance tuition.

Numerous articles in dance magazines and media around the world written by dance professionals and dance medicine/science experts over recent years draw attention to these problems. One of ballet's biggest stars—Diana Vishneva—has warned that the development of young ballerinas is being jeopardised by viral videos of hyper-elastic dancers performing incredible tricks.

Young ballet stars being ruined by Instagram, says Russian prima ballerina Diana Vishneva
"Often I see young dancers more interested in their phones than what is going on in rehearsals," said the star of the Mariinsky Ballet in Saint Petersburg, the birthplace of Tchaikovsky's "The Nutcracker" and "The Sleeping Beauty".

[…]

"They see the surface, the great bodies, but they don't realise the work behind that," said the former star pupil of the legendary Vaganova Academy, the school that produced Nijinsky, Nureyev, Anna Pavlova and Natalia Makarova.

[…]

"They don't know about timing or have a sense of movement. It has to happen right away. They want everything now."

(The Telegraph, 1 October 2018)

ABC journalists Lesley Robinson and Sarah Whyte posted this article on ABC News:

> **Dancers injured copying overstretching exercises from social media**
> Young dancers are being injured copying extreme overstretching exercises they have seen online, a trend that medical professionals say could ruin their careers.
>
> Images of dancers overstretching their legs and hips have flooded Instagram and YouTube, in positions called the "scorpion" and "over split leg mount", which forces the leg behind the head.
>
> Dance physiotherapist Lisa Howell urged dancers not to copy pictures and videos shared online, after seeing a spike in hip and back injuries in dancers aged 11 to 14.
>
> She said children were pushing their bodies beyond their physical limits.
>
> "Now we're seeing labral tears (tear in hip joint) and issues in their back in 11 and 12-year-olds, which is very disconcerting because while they're doing these moves to make themselves better dancers, they are often actually ruling themselves out

of a professional career because they are getting injuries so young," Ms Howell said.

The trend has meant inexperienced dancers are trying to imitate complicated gymnastic moves performed by highly trained gymnasts.

'The biggest issue we have now is that people are taking moves from rhythmic gymnasts and trying to insert them into dance and trying to do this in a very, very quick way as a one stop shop, rather than looking at all of the detailed training that has to go in before any of those tricks are actually attempted,' she said. […]

The risk of injury is also growing as the popularity of dance surges. […]

Dancers sharing the images are often from the United States and Australia and have hundreds of thousands of followers online.

Young dancers are also publishing 'how to' videos on YouTube, showing how to do advanced gymnastics stretching.

Marko Panzic, who runs the prestigious Dream Dance Company, said the social media trend was leading towards a 'dangerous side of dance'.

'It just makes me go ouch,' he said.

'It's not something that I look at and go, "Wow, that's amazing"'.

Two promising Australian dancers have spoken out against the growing trend, saying their injuries could have been avoided if they did not push themselves into such extreme positions.

'Those pictures on Instagram, they physically make me ill because I know that that's not what your body should be able to do,' 18-year-old Aaron Matheson said.

Aaron was practicing a scorpion, or a back mount, at home when he first injured himself seven years ago.

'I just kept trying every day I got home after dancing and eventually I finally got it, but I also felt my back twinge when I did it and I just had to collapse to the ground and just wait until the pain was gone,' Aaron said.

He is now being treated for a stress fracture.

Charlotte Connors, 17, from Newcastle, injured herself trying to copy a YouTube video at home. […]

Both dancers wish they had known what kind of long-term damage could be ahead of them, before attempting extreme overstretching.

'It can either make you or break you as a dancer,' Aaron said.

'If you're going to push yourself so far while you're young, you're not going to have a future when you're older.

'And kids need to learn that now, sooner than later.'

'If you feel pain stop, because the pain is the brain's message; please stop what you're doing because it's wrong,' she said.

(12 October 2015, updated 22 January 2016)

Safeguarding your child against the unethical, dangerous training methods that are causing physical damage to students worldwide nowadays means your child will not be subjected to physical injury and psychological abuse. Without information and guidance at your fingertips, the job of finding a safe dance studio that employs genuinely qualified and trained teachers is like finding a needle in a haystack. Your child deserves more than just 'potluck'.

Children enrolled in dance classes should be learning to dance—not to be contortionists.

Alarm bells ring when we read articles like this:

> **Making all the wrong moves? Australia's dance industry under scrutiny:**
> *Dance is among the most popular activities for young Australians, but is their wellbeing in danger?*
>
> [...] 'tricks' from an increasingly Americanised dance scene, which borrows heavily from pageant culture and advanced gymnastics, and is fuelled by television shows *Dance Moms* and *So You Think You Can Dance*, have prompted dance medicine experts to warn of high injury risks.
>
> 'I know kids who are pushing and pushing every day to hyperextend,' Tina says. Training for hyperextension can involve a young dancer doing the splits on the floor with her feet lifted on brick-sized blocks. 'How will this affect her when she is 30 or carrying a baby?'
>
> Paul Malek, a prominent dance school owner in Melbourne, worked as a choreographer on *So You Think You Can Dance Australia* and says young girls are 'training like 18- to 20-year-old gymnasts, risking injury to their hips and lower spine and risking not being able to walk when they are 30 [...]'
>
> (Chris Johnston, *Sydney Morning Herald*, 8 July 2015)

It's unbelievable that in this day and age, with so much scientific/ medical knowledge in dance and exercise science, that there are teachers who are teaching dangerous stretching to young dance students.

With over forty years' experience as a dance professional, I have seen dance from many angles—as a dance teacher, adjudicator, professional dancer/performer in many genres, choreographer, director, mentor, student and parent of a professional ballet dancer. Together with fellow dance professionals I have been increasingly concerned, and sometimes shocked and horrified, over the way in which many vulnerable parents and their children are being misled, injured and exploited as dance studios and various competitions and conventions profit. I am not a professor or an academic. I don't hold myself up on a pedestal professing to know everything about dance. I don't. But I've been 'boots on the ground' in dance tuition, performing, teaching, adjudicating etc., since the age of sixteen. I have written this book as a guide for all dance parents and students, out of a sense of responsibility and to urge you all to become better informed about the dance world and what you are subjecting your children to. Together with my colleagues and dance experts, I want you to be able to find the best teachers and the best (which also means the safest) studios for your children.

Confused and sometimes distraught parents by the dozens have contacted me searching for advice and answers. I have written this book to address the problems facing dance parents and students today, bringing together information from many sources and from my own extensive experience, in an endeavour to provide some guidance for parents, who are often sailing through the rough seas of the dance world without a compass.

After reading this book you will be armed with the knowledge to lead your child's greatest opportunities for success. Knowing what to look for and what to look out for, you and particularly your child will be less likely to fall prey to unsatisfactory situations. You will be able to carefully guide your child's dance education journey, whether they enjoy recreational classes or aspire to a professional dance career.

The worldwide dance industry is huge with a massive and growing number of privately-run performing arts studios that offer almost every dance style. This book is not about the highly esteemed establishments, which are often attached to ballet or dance companies (or the schools that feed into them). It's not about any particular type of studio or training. It is about the worldwide global issues in the dance industry that are affecting children who learn dancing (and their families)—many of whom, I'm afraid, are being led up the garden path and ripped off.

CHAPTER 1

Problem One – Anyone Can Open a Dance Studio and Teach Dancing

Alarmingly, anyone can open a dance studio and teach dancing, without a licence or qualification or registration. The dance industry is not regulated. There is no regulator. Experts agree that dance is probably the largest unregulated industry involving children.

Dance teachers and dance studio owners do not have to answer to a governing body, or licensing organisation. If a studio is doing the wrong thing, there is nowhere for parents to make a complaint. No one is held accountable.

You will be surprised to know there is no 'consumer watchdog' for the booming dance industry.

No mandatory qualifications are required. No one needs a licence to teach dance or to set up a dance studio. Dance studios operate in isolation and there are no national or international standards. Attempts by several organisations to create governing bodies for dance over the years have all been unsuccessful.

In Australia there are organisations such as Ausdance. New Zealand has DANZ. In the UK there is One Dance UK, and in the USA there is the National Dance Education Organization (NDEO). Such

PROBLEM ONE – *Anyone Can Open a Dance Studio and Teach Dancing*

organisations as these provide online resources for teachers, parents and studios, but they have no licensing, governing authority or regulatory power over dance teachers or studios. Many parents are not even aware of these organisations. It would be helpful if dance studios included information about them on their websites.

Teachers do not need qualifications or experience to teach dance. There are no certificates required and no standardised procedures that need to be followed. 'Joe Bloggs', the plumber from down the road, could open a dance studio if he wanted to. He could also teach dance!

Almost all industries are regulated, except dance.

In netball all coaches are accredited and registered with their state and national governing bodies. All calisthenics clubs are registered with a state body. Gymnastics Australia coaches must be accredited and registered. The fitness industry is regulated, as is after-school care. Tertiary institutions offer degree courses and certificates for those wishing to teach in the public sector (high schools and colleges), but no courses or certificates are required for private studios. There appear to be many unqualified, inexperienced teachers operating and much damage can be done to young dance students if these unqualified teachers are not supervised by fully qualified teachers.

As you read on you will realise why it's so important that you find teachers who teach an international or nationally recognised syllabus, as this will ensure that they are qualified and certified and registered in that particular syllabus.

The only requirement is that all staff and visiting teachers who work in a dance studio must have a Blue Card (working with children clearance), as does anyone at all coming into the studio to do maintenance and repairs etc. However, these are not enforced and often not checked.

We all know that, as in any field, there are good businesses, bad businesses, and everything in between. Dance is no exception.

Dance is big business and the big question is: Do some studios/teachers place more importance on profits than they do on the overall care and wellbeing of the students? In my experience, the answer is an unequivocal yes.

You would be amazed to find that more children are learning to dance now than ever before, which is great news, especially for dance studio owners. There are around 6,000 dance studios in Australia, and around 53,000 in the USA.

According to the Bureau of Statistics, dance is the second most popular activity for young people, after swimming, with more than half a million children and young people taking part in some sort of dance education in Australia.

This number is increasing by tens of thousands each year and swells with the inclusion of children under five years of age and over fourteen years of age. In the USA, the Dance Studies Industry has experienced growth of 3.5 per cent over the five years to 2018 with revenue of up to US$3.6 billion (source www.ibisworld.com).

Until quite recently, dance teachers never expected to really 'make' any money from teaching and were lucky to make ends meet. They taught because they loved the art of dance and loved helping children learn. Now it's big business, with large-scale studios sometimes seeming to be super-focused on profits.

Dance tuition and competitions appear to be getting quite a tarnished reputation in the community nowadays.

Look before You Leap—or Gamble on a Blind Leap of Faith?

As parents we drop our children off at dance classes and we like to think that all is well, but we must ask these questions:

- Do I really know what's going on in my child's dance classes?
- Is my child being taught properly and safely?
- Who is teaching my child and are they qualified?

There are top-quality dance studios that offer highly qualified, extremely knowledgeable, dedicated, genuinely professional and experienced teachers. There is also the opposite. Unqualified, unknowledgeable, unprofessional people may appear to be qualified and professional to naïve parents who may be led to believe that a Certificate III or IV in dance qualifies the person to teach. It doesn't.

It is amazing to observe the advertising strategies and ploys that are available and used now that can create such a powerful illusion (not just

PROBLEM ONE – Anyone Can Open a Dance Studio and Teach Dancing

in dance). Clever advertising can create a brand so convincingly that parents and students can't see past the smoke and mirrors to realise there may be little substance behind the image.

When parents have little, or no knowledge, of dance, they can be exploited and taken advantage of. They can be 'sitting ducks'—easy targets for selling and upselling to.

How can parents find dancing classes for their children that are run ethically by high-quality, true professionals? Advertising, especially social media advertising, is often exaggerated, misleading and unreliable as the necessity to cover high overheads and make a profit becomes the focus. For example, taglines in advertising in which businesses may profess to be 'the best' when they are actually mainly employing student teachers are misleading. They operate more like production lines with a high turnover of students (and teachers). Colleagues agree that parents and students must have access to information that will lead them to find safe and successful dance training for their children.

How can parents look beyond the superficial picture that is painted by social media platforms and online advertising? Read on and you will learn how.

We dance professionals are aware that there have been many changes in the teaching of the art of dance over the years. Development and change are inevitable and much of it is good progress. However, over the past fifteen years or so a growing number of big problems have emerged or grown worse, big in the sense of unethical, disturbing, dishonest and even dangerous and damaging. Experts agree that these problems are negatively impacting dance students and their families. They include the following:

- The dance industry is not regulated.
- There is a lack of duty of care.
- There is a worldwide epidemic of unethical training, overtraining and extreme stretching.
- Parents and students lack the knowledge to make good decisions.
- There has been an increase in injuries in dance students.
- The global sexualisation of dance students is extremely concerning.
- There is a plethora of unqualified, inexperienced teachers.

- There is insufficient information accessible to parents/caregivers and students.
- Much advertising is misleading.
- Child protection policies and procedures are inadequate and there is a lack of transparency in studios—for example, a lack of viewing windows or live video feeds of classes.

Every child who learns dancing deserves top-quality training and a happy, safe and rewarding dance education. When parents are educated, informed and empowered they can be guaranteed to make intelligent decisions about dance training from 'baby' dance to the pre-professional dancer.

Educators, dance/science experts and medical professionals share my concerns regarding how unethically young dancers are being trained in some studios, though we believe the majority of teachers are well-intentioned. Incidences of children crying from the pain inflicted on them by extreme overstretching methods should not be allowed and must be stopped. Stories of children under the age of thirteen years dancing for over twelve hours in one day with virtually no breaks are totally unacceptable. Many examples of unacceptable situations must be stopped, such as young dance students having to rehearse and perform for over twenty hours in one weekend and then commence the week again first thing Monday morning with no break for the body and mind to rest and recover. Teachers who inflict this type of situation on their students may say that it's okay because professional dancers have to dance for many hours each day. But there's a massive difference: these are students—not professional dancers! There is a huge difference in training students who are at varying developmental ages/stages and managing a group of professional dancers. There is no comparison.

We have a responsibility and duty to draw attention to these problems so parents are aware of them and can protect their children from harm.

We take our hats off to the dedicated, hard-working expert dance professionals whom we wish all dance parents and students will find in the midst of all the social media 'spin'. We feel very concerned that so many parents and students are being inadvertently or intentionally misled and misinformed.

PROBLEM ONE – *Anyone Can Open a Dance Studio and Teach Dancing*

The true professional dance studios are exemplary in all facets mentioned and it is imperative that parents know what to look for so they can find these fantastic studios. Such studios have the best interests of the students at heart—not the profits.

A shiny, rosy, specially waxed apple on the outside may be rotten on the inside. Businesses, including dance studio businesses, can be the same. The dance studio that your child attends may not be all that it appears to be and putting your trust and your money into something you know very little about is very risky.

It is of great importance for you to know how to find the best path for your child's dance education, so it is not just a blind leap of faith.

The Parent–Teacher Tug of War

In today's world many people want everything instantly, but no-one can wave a magic wand and turn a child into a dancer. Some (pseudo) teachers can convince an unknowledgeable parent that they can make their child into a star sooner rather than later. However, it takes many years of learning each level of a training system. Never believe anyone who tells you your child is brilliant or a 'star' or 'stunning', or that they are destined for fame and fortune. No genuine teacher would come out with such verbal diarrhoea. Often the intention is to pander to the unsuspecting parents in order to extract as much money as possible out of them.

By the same token, teachers must not allow themselves to be bullied by ambitious and stubborn parents who want instant success and 'fame' for their children. Teachers must not run their studios catering to what they think the parents want so they can retain and attract more students. Ethics and integrity are key.

Quality, Not Quantity

The advice that is often fed to dance students and their parents that to be successful they must take more and more classes in every style of dance is utterly false. Performing a step several times to a high standard is much more beneficial than bashing through it twenty times with sloppy technique. Pushing dance students too fast, too young only creates physical and psychological damage and burnout. It takes at least twelve years to train a dancer. There is no 'fast fix' and no reason for children to be rushed through their training. Steer clear of any online advertising that promises to make your child into a 'star' quickly. Dance can be very expensive but there is no need for parents to pay more than is necessary for a successful dance education.

Expert teachers are banging their heads against a wall as they lose students to studios whose priority is largely winning competitions. They try to make the students into mini-professional-like 'stars' at a young age by using dangerous and age-inappropriate training methods, often taught by unqualified teachers. There is absolutely nothing to be gained by being 'pushed' in this way. But there is an awful lot to lose.

Fethon Miozzi, ballet teacher of the middle and senior classes in the Vaganova Ballet Academy of St Petersburg, had this to say recently:

> **How to develop in the right way young talents in the ballet?**
> In recent times, I often come across many videos of young aspiring dancers, even from the age of six, who, in various competitions or performances, they dance the most famous variations of the prima ballerina from the classical repertory.
>
> It is always nice to see the enthusiasm with which young dancers perform the solos, but I personally do not really support that young children perform such complex variations at this young age. Of course, there are also cases where children can easily perform technical difficulties, but in most cases this is a very dangerous task, which often leads to irreparable physical injuries.
>
> Another important point is that the task of the teacher is also to make the child understand the importance of the goal, which must be achieved through hard physical work. If you start from the finish line, what will motivate a young student to start all over again with a 'plié' facing to the barre?

PROBLEM ONE – *Anyone Can Open a Dance Studio and Teach Dancing*

Obviously in high professional schools such as our Vaganova Ballet Academy, this is never done, and the study of ballet is gradual depending on the age, preparation and program to be followed every year. But in many schools around the world, where parental ambitions often take over, this process is not followed. The task therefore of the teacher in this case would be, in addition to creating choreographies appropriate to the age of the young pupils, also to make parents understand that the health of the child is the most important thing and that, for example, to put point shoes on at an early age, involves serious complications.

So please, don't try to perform *Odette* or *Giselle* just born, everything has to happen in due time.

Always go step by step so as not to spoil your children!

Undoubtedly, it is important to teach the young students a general knowledge of ballet and try to interest them in this magnificent art, but you need to do it right and understand what is possible and what is impossible!

(Facebook, 18 June 2020)

CHAPTER 2

Problem Two – The Alarming Rise in Injuries Among Dance Students

According to Kathleen McGuire, 'There is a flexibility freak show going on in the dance world' (Danceteacher.com, March 2018), and Chris Johnson of the *Sydney Morning Herald* wrote on 8 July 2015:

> Physiotherapists worldwide are reporting an alarming rise in injuries that are not normally associated with dance.
>
> According to Sydney physiotherapist Debra Crookshanks, who is on the board of the International Association of Dance Medicine and Science, overtraining is rife, because competitions and eisteddfods are fierce, and kids come to her with advanced injuries. A study by Melinda Purnell, a University of Sydney PhD student Crookshanks supervised, based on data from 2008, found a 'chronic' risk of injury for dancers aged under 14 who were doing more than 8.5 hours training a week.
>
> But it is injuries the industry is talking about the loudest. These are most common in either untrained dancers who try extreme moves seen on social media or, more commonly, elite dancers aged 12 to 14 who are doing up to 30 hours week in training and competitions.

PROBLEM TWO – The Alarming Rise in Injuries Among Dance Students

> 'The competition kids,' Purnell says, 'these are injuries previously only seen in professional dancers.' She cites hip cartilage damage and stress fractures as increasing and cites a trend of turning dancers into 'contortionists'.
>
> The danger age range for high risk of injuries through overtraining is 11 to 15, she says.

Well-meaning parents believe their children are receiving the best dancing training, until the unthinkable happens.

The following is a shocking and sickening true story of an injury to a young child at her recreational jazz dance class at a studio on the Gold Coast, Australia. It is written by the family's lawyer and published with the family's permission. Imagine if this was your daughter!

> She was 7 years of age at the time of her injury. Her teacher was assisting her by placing pressure and repositioning her legs to achieve a further split (forced flexion) when she felt a lot of pain in her hip. When she left the class she was visibly in pain and upset. Two days post seeing a doctor for limping and pain in her hip, her condition worsened, and she developed weakness in the legs until she was unable to walk. She did not walk again for three and a half weeks.
>
> She was hospitalised and diagnosed with Functional Neurological Dysfunction. Her symptoms included: tics, tremors, paralysis, severe limb weakness, severe fatigue and pain. The physical and psychological impact of this technique on this young child was traumatic and she required intensive physiotherapy and psychology sessions to assist in her recovery. She still struggles with pain at times and has fears associated with stretching.
>
> Studies have identified that people with Functional Neurological Dysfunction have a higher level of childhood stressors such as emotional neglect, sexual abuse and physical abuse compared to controls (Ludwig et al., 2018).

This is a horrifying story and is not an isolated incident. This sort of incident should never happen to dance students. Dangerous forms of stretching must be stopped. We are starting to hear of injuries to students under the age of eighteen requiring hip replacements and arthroscopy operations from being forcibly overstretched into positions that are past their range of flexibility. For example, astoundingly damaging to children are the exercises where their feet are up on blocks or stretching ladders while the teacher pushes them down into an over-split. Or ghastly hoist-like stretching bands are hung over doors and hooked over feet and the child (with no supervision) hoists the leg up as high as possible. The chance of achieving any improvement in any way is zero and the chance of serious damage to the child very high.

Stop Chasing the 'WOW' Factor

Children do not have to be able to put their legs around their necks or turn themselves 'inside out' in order to enjoy dancing and be successful at it. There is far too much emphasis on increasing children's flexibility nowadays. Mimicking gymnastics or acrobatics is not dancing. Teachers must stop trying to create the short-term 'WOW' factor at the expense of children. Parents must stop being impressed by the instant 'shock and awe' of tricks and dangerous methods of teaching and performing.

Much more attention needs to be paid to quality of movement, genuine safe technique and expressing the music and emotion with style and artistry, since dance is an art form and not a sport.

There is something seriously wrong in the industry, for instance, when a parent asks if her eight-year-old daughter should be crying in class from the pain of being 'stretched' by teachers and students pushing her body into extreme positions. The child was having trouble walking and relied on taking Nurofen for several days for pain relief! The best way to prevent these injuries is to make sure your child learns from fully qualified, registered, experienced and knowledgeable teachers.

As guest of the Vaganova Academy of Classical Ballet in St Petersburg, Russia, I was privileged to meet with the then Director

PROBLEM TWO – The Alarming Rise in Injuries Among Dance Students

Vera Dorofeeva. Through a translator, she told me the Academy does not let the children stretch between the ages of ten and fourteen years because it ruins their hips and by the age of twenty-eight years they won't be able to dance. 'We know what we are doing. We have been doing this for over 400 years!' she said. The renowned vocational schools around the world do not 'stretch' (or overstretch) the students—they strengthen them.

> Many people advocating extreme training have no idea of the long-term trouble they may be causing … Every day in my role as a Physiotherapist I see people suffering from old injuries sustained by over stretching, repeated extensions and excessively mobile and unstable joints from early training.
>
> (Lisa Howell, *Perfect Form Physiotherapy*, theballetblog.com)

Experts cannot understand why some studio owners have so much power that parents appear to put their protective instincts aside and go along with unethical practices, even when their children are suffering.

It appears that the desire to win competitions at any cost, to be 'Insta-famous', and to imitate the *Dance Moms* culture is so strong that parents are ignoring scientific proof (if they are even aware of it) that what their children are being subjected to can be very damaging. We must never put our children's bodies at risk in order to win trophies or to entertain others.

Ambitious and sometimes ruthless studio directors and teachers can be so driven to achieve success that they seem to steamroll parents and students into doing what they're told, without question and at the expense of the children. Children are afraid to speak up in case they get into trouble and parents are afraid to speak up in case their child suffers the consequences (being overlooked for solo parts or put in the back row of the concert dance as punishment, or being verbally abused—yes, this does happen). As parents, we want to believe our children are in safe hands, but unfortunately this is not always the case.

The advancements in dance medicine and scientific research are proof of the dangers to dance students worldwide. Overall, there appears to be an enormous gap in knowledge of safe dance practice between the professional dance world and the amateur world of the local dance studio, which may employ junior or student teachers (unsupervised), and which have no idea what visiting teachers are teaching the students.

The Worldwide Epidemic of Dangerous Stretching and Overtraining

Children who are not physically gifted for dance sometimes feel inferior and lose confidence and self-esteem when, for instance, the teacher praises students who are naturally flexible. This is sad as there is a lot more to dance than flexibility and all children who dance have something to offer as a student dancer. The students who possess natural flexibility and hyperextension endure their own set of problems as they must work hard to control and stabilise their joints. Students must be informed that the importance of being hyperflexible has been tragically overstated and will not make them a better dancer. A certain amount of flexibility is desirable in a dancer and you won't see a professional dancer who has poor flexibility. But it must be remembered that these are dance STUDENTS and have varying body types and physical attributes. Much more time and energy need to be spent on developing technique, quality of movement and steps, movement transitions, musicality, coordination, ports de bras and epaulement (in ballet) dynamics, expression, interpretation, and artistry. There is an absurd amount of time and energy spent on stretching in dance lessons now.

If a studio is running 'stretch and technique' classes, parents should thoroughly look into what exactly is being taught. Parents should also check if there's any stretching being done in their recreational dance classes. Children must be educated on safe stretching and safe training and learn to speak up and tell the teacher they are not allowed to do overstretching or extreme stretching.

Extreme overstretching and dangerous forms of stretching have become worldwide epidemics. Just because it is being done everywhere does not mean it's the right thing to do.

Parents must seek professional advice from doctors and physiotherapists if their child complains of pain and investigate thoroughly what the child is being subjected to at their dance studio. Children must not be afraid to speak up and they must be taken seriously.

Do not ignore your child's complaints or tell your child to toughen up. The old adage of 'no pain, no gain' is a myth. Do not let the teacher or studio owner dismiss your concerns.

Parents and students—some of whom may be new to the world of dance—may not know what to expect or may not know what 'safe stretching' is.

It's important that parents and children know what they should and should not be doing when it comes to stretching. Teachers are accountable and responsible for safe dance practices in their studios and classes—that is, practices that minimise the risk of injury to their students. Parents are responsible for making sure their children don't try dangerous movements at home and at the studio. So parents need to become better educated and informed about the different forms of stretching.

No child should have their bodies or legs forced into positions beyond their normal range of motion (ROM) by teachers or fellow students.

Many children will have physical problems as they mature as a result of poor practices. Little research has been done into the long-term results of dangerous stretching methods and overtraining as the epidemic has spread so quickly around the world in recent years. The physical damage done to children will have serious effects on their lives later on. The children whose bodies are not suited to being subjected to this type of unethical training are most at risk as their bodies are forced past their normal range of movement. Injuries sustained through overtraining, overuse, overstretching (extreme overstretching), and attempting to perform steps and movements that are too advanced for the age and stage of the child's development can prevent them from going on to potential careers in the performing arts.

Children everywhere try to copy dangerous positions from Instagram and other social media platforms. Unfortunately, some teachers encourage the students and incorporate these positions and movements into classes and dance routines. Students who are naturally hypermobile do not need to practise more overstretching; they need to build strength in order to stabilise their joints.

Dr Nick Cutri (Los Angeles), who has a doctorate in physical therapy and a fellowship in applied functional science, is alarmed by the numbers of young dancers with chronic injuries. Writing in *Dance Magazine*, Emma Sandall quoted him as saying:

> An 8-year-old should never have orthopaedic pain. We are seeing 8–15-year-olds who have neurologically oriented back pain and spine compression that will never get better.
>
> (27 January 2020)

There are safe training methods that educated, well-qualified and experienced teachers use to increase flexibility in dance students. It is of great importance that parents find these teachers for their child as their child only has one body and needs to learn to respect and look after it. Not all injuries in growing bodies can be fixed.

> In young students whose bones are not fully developed there is also a serious risk of damaging the shape of the hip socket, or developing spinal stress fractures or Spondylolisthesis. If a joint is pushed past its normal range of motion there is a risk of damaging the surrounding tissues, including the labrum of

the hip and the ligaments that surround the joint. Long term, over-stretched joints carry a higher risk of developing arthritic changes due to wear and tear.

(Lisa Howell, dance physiotherapist, theballetblog.com)

Have the standards gotten out of control? The truth is it depends on the body. 'Some people are genetically predisposed to that kind of flexibility', says Leigh Heflin, formerly of Harkness Center for Dance Injuries at New York University's Langone Medical Center.

There have been a growing number of injuries in dance students under the age of sixteen in recent years. Why is this a bad thing and why should we be concerned? Because:

1. Some of these injuries will prevent students from pursuing a career in dance.
2. A short-term goal should never be at the expense of a possible long-term hobby or career.
3. Many injuries are the result of overtraining and/or overuse, incorrect teaching or technique, unsuitable floors (e.g. hard or slippery).
4. Such injuries as torn groins, torn ligaments, nerve damage in backs, hip impingements and so on will cause the students problems and pain later in life.
5. Some of the injuries we are seeing now in children are not repairable.
6. These injuries are unnecessary and largely avoidable.
7. Children should not be subjected to pain or be in increased danger of injury.
8. Parents must avoid schools that encourage children to 'work through the pain'.
9. Although a certain amount of flexibility is desirable for dancers, it should never be forced.
10. Strength is more desirable than flexibility.
11. Being extremely flexible doesn't mean you are a good dancer.

Recreational dance classes should never involve overstretching, extreme stretching or 'hands-on' stretching or 'partner' stretching. Parents must be informed by the teacher and studio if any of these forms of stretching are to be done in the class.

Warming Up is Not Stretching

In order to minimise the risk of injury in dance students, teachers must make sure the students have enough time to warm up properly.

When a dance student is told to 'warm up' before a class and then left to their own ideas, they will often stretch. Many will sit in the 'frog' position, attempt splits and leg mounts etc. However, this is not the correct way to warm up. Stretching before a class decreases the ability of your muscles to work well, by reducing balance, endurance, strength, speed, and jumping ability for up to an hour.

Purpose of warming up

The role of stretching during a warm-up is to mobilise muscles and prepare them safely to carry out the range of motion required of dance activities, not to increase flexibility.

A warm-up generally consists of three or four sections: a gentle pulse-raising section, a joint-mobilising section, a muscle-lengthening section, and sometimes a second pulse-raising section).[1] The pulse-raising sections aim to increase cardiorespiratory and metabolic rates; these are the prerequisite to all further activity. The joint-mobilising section consists of gently moving the various joints through their ranges of motion, and the purpose of the muscle-lengthening section is to prepare the muscles for the demands to come through the use of dynamic stretching.[2]

Of course the type of warm-up depends on the style of dance class you are doing. So a hip-hop dancer may do a slightly different warm-up to a ballet dancer. There is no set warm-up and many

---

[1] Quin, E, Rafferty S & Tomlinson, C 2015, *Safe dance practice: An applied dance science perspective*, Human Kinetics Publishers.
[2] Wilmerding, MV & Krasnow, DH (eds) 2017, *Dancer wellness*, International Association for Dance Medicine & Science. Human Kinetics.

PROBLEM TWO – The Alarming Rise in Injuries Among Dance Students

different variations, but a suggested standard warm-up should consist of the following:

1. Raising the body temperature and heart rate and blood flow by light jogging, or astride jumps (in proper running shoes to avoid stress on the Achilles tendons) for one to five minutes. This is probably not practical for dance students who are in hour-long classes with little time for changing shoes. So light jogging on the spot, brisk walking, skipping around the room, pony gallops and such like can be effective, and the children love doing them.
2. Mobilise all major joints and the spine with exercises like roll ups, roll downs, ankle circles, stretching and flexing through the feet; arm circles, shoulder rolls, hip circles lying on your back on the floor.
3. Lengthen the muscles and gauge balance, posture, alignment and core stability. (Use a BOSU ball for strength and balance if available.) Lengthening the muscles is not stretching them and you should not go past your range of movement in the warm-up. Stretches that are held for less than fifteen seconds are beneficial, but a dance student should not hold a stretch in the warm-up for longer than that as it causes the muscles to destabilise.

Cooling down

A 'cool-down' should always be done at the end of each class or rehearsal. It can help your body to recover.

The aim of the cool-down is to get the body's temperature and heart rate back to normal and reduce the amount of lactic acid in the body as this is what causes soreness and stiffness. Slow movements such as grands port de bras, big arm movements combined with concentrating on breathing and gentle stretches into such things as lunges, as well as floor stretches, can be effective cool-down techniques. Deep stretches should only be undertaken if the dancer has no more classes or rehearsals that day. Always make sure you move slowly in and out of positions during the cool-down as the heart rate is lowered gradually.

What is Stretching, Overstretching and Extreme Stretching?

Up until about twenty years ago having high extensions and being super flexible was quite rare in dancers. It certainly was not the 'norm'. Going back even further than that, it was considered a 'high leg' when a dancer's leg was at a 90-degree angle to the body. There were certainly exceptions to that rule, but the emphasis was always on 'line'—that is, aesthetically pleasing positions, style and artistry, not to mention grace and elegance. To me, these priorities went hand in hand beautifully with classical ballet and the short classical tutus and other ballet costumes. Even in 'modern dance', flexibility wasn't really a 'thing' at all. The dancers seemed to be strong and many had rather long careers—notably, Prima Ballerina Maya Plisetskaya, who was born in 1925 and performed with the Bolshoi Ballet Company until 1990. Similarly, Dame Margot Fonteyn performed with the Royal Ballet for forty-five years. Many ballerinas and male dancers of that time had long careers. Of course, they didn't do any extreme stretching in those days.

It's a different story now! High extensions in ballet are now desirable, and contemporary, modern and jazz dance have evolved and changed, as have the expectations placed on dancers who pursue professional careers. For example, a dancer who is gifted in classical ballet must also be highly skilled in contemporary dance in order to be considered for entry into a ballet company. The demands put on professional dancers in this day and age are largely due to the choreography they are expected to perform.

Once a dancer reaches this professional level they have a firm grasp on all facets of their dance abilities, including strengths and weaknesses and future potential. Some company directors have commented that they are seeing some weaknesses in dancers due to an imbalance in their training. More and more dancers coming into a company have a high chance of injury because they have spent too much time on increasing their flexibility and not enough on building their strength.

PROBLEM TWO – The Alarming Rise in Injuries Among Dance Students

Their joints are sometimes hypermobile and unsteady. This was not the case some years ago.

Sadly, many students who constantly overstretch past their natural ROM (range of motion) in a forced manner and attempt extreme movements during training never have a chance to even audition for professional jobs due to the injuries they sustain and the long-term repercussions.

> Dancers are known for their extreme flexibility, but can you take it too far? The answer is yes. In the social media world we live in, we are exposing children to images of stretches that almost seem inhuman. Dance teachers are often cautious about taking on such practices but feel pressured to keep up with the times by both students and parents. However, erring on the side of caution is not a bad thing. The possible dangers that exist with over stretching are high. Training young adolescents is much different than training adults; it is important your dance teacher is aware of the possible dangers that exist and how to prevent them in young dancers.
>
> (Shannon Thomas, *Dance Life*, 27 July 2015)

Strange but true: The main problem with overstretching is that your muscle fibers aren't the only things getting longer. That's because forcing your muscles into an extreme stretch also forces ligaments and joint capsules to lengthen, and these connective tissues don't benefit from being stretched. "Stretched-out ligaments lose their ability to contract back to their original length," Richardson explains. "And joint capsules are like little balloons that hold our joints in place. Once that balloon or ligament is stretched out, your muscles have to work harder to create stability—which isn't their job."

If your muscles are busy stabilizing your joints, they can't produce as much force (think lower jumps, slower response times, and more muscle fatigue). Not to mention that joint instability from incorrect stretching can lead to injuries, including hip impingement, evulsion fractures, and labral tears.

(Helen Rolfe, *Dance Spirit*, 18 October 2019)

Some dancers and dance students are naturally very flexible; others are not. The dancers who are very flexible have to work on strengthening their bodies in order to control this flexibility so that they are able to increase their joint stability and reduce the chance of injury. Dancers who are not naturally flexible can improve safely by using strengthening methods that balance stretching with strength.

Knowing the Different Types of Stretching

Ballistic stretch

Many dance movements are ballistic. A ballistic stretch is when, for instance, the leg is swung upwards in a high-leg kick or grand battement. It is not held at the height of the movement but swings back down. Propelled by the momentum of the leg, it creates a force that in turn creates the 'stretch'. There can be some short-term improvements to flexibility by performing ballistic stretches, but because it is not a controlled movement there is an increase in the chance of injury. Ballistic movements should only be done when the dancer is fully warmed up.

Dynamic stretch

Dynamic stretches are controlled dance-stretching exercises that engage many joints and prepare the dancer for what they will be doing onstage and in class. A good example of a dynamic stretch is a developpe, or battement fondu in ballet, where the dancer will endeavour to reach as much height as possible. This type of stretching should also only be done when the dancer is fully warmed up.

Static stretch

A static stretch is held for thirty seconds during which time the muscle is being elongated to its maximum. There should be no pain. The same stretch should be repeated three or four times with relaxation in between. There will be a feeling of the muscle being stretched, but under no circumstances should there be any sharp pain or pain of any sort. If done properly and in a controlled way, static stretches are effective and unlikely to cause damage.

Prolonged stretch

This type of stretch should be avoided as it can lead to loss of stability and serious injury. Prolonged stretches are similar to static stretches but are held in the position for much longer, for several minutes in fact. You may see dancers sitting on the floor in the splits or side splits for instance for many minutes; however, this can contribute to future injury as it causes unnecessary compression of the hip labrum.

Proprioceptive Neuromuscular Facilitation (PNF)

PNF techniques involve contracting and relaxing opposite muscle groups and each of the many types of PNF-stretching techniques have three phases (hold–relax, contract–relax, hold–relax with agonist contraction).

PNF techniques shouldn't be undertaken without the guidance of a doctor or physiotherapist as they can cause injury and must be performed correctly to avoid this risk.

Overstretching and extreme stretching

These forms of stretching should NEVER be done in a dance studio or at home. They are not safe forms of stretching. Any form of stretching that involves a student's body being forced by themselves, a teacher, a fellow student, or a stretching apparatus into a position that is well beyond their normal ROM is very dangerous. Students sitting on other students' bodies and students standing on other students' legs to force them down in the frog position etc. are all extreme forms of overstretching and must not be done. They are very dangerous and *will* cause injury.

The International Association of Dance Medicine & Science gives this advice on when to stretch:

Stretching is not the same as warming up. The purpose of a warm-up is to increase the temperature of the core and muscle tissue. An indication that the body temperature has increased is a slight sweat appearing on the skin. The time prior to class should not be used to increase flexibility. Warm muscles are more extensible and responsive, so it is far better to stretch immediately AFTER class or rehearsal when muscles have been exercised for 1–2 hours. Research has shown that applying a small amount of stretch force to warm connective tissues lengthened them more effectively than larger stretch forces (four times larger) applied to the same tissues at normal body temperature. Long-term retention of tissue length lasted more than twice as long when the low-load stretch was applied to warm tissue. Additionally, stretching with higher tissue temperatures, as seen following class or rehearsal, resulted in fewer injuries. Holding the stretch while cooling down allows even greater increases in tissue length to be achieved.

Dance is Art—Tricks Are Tricks

As parents and students are increasingly being sucked into the Americanised, achievement-based competitive dance scene, they are buying into the 'hype' created by the dance studio ethos and social media.

We are concerned that some dance education is becoming more and more like competitive sport and less like performing art. Like fast food, it's convenient, looks good on the surface, gives instant satisfaction, has short-term benefits, makes big profits for the company. Like fast food, the long-term effects are bad for your health.

Another fact that needs to be kept in mind is this: the art of dance uses movement to communicate meaning about the human experience. It is far more than exercise or entertainment. Dance is not cheerleading, gymnastics or contortion. Dance has soul!

Dragging the 'art' of dance down is the inclusion of 'tricks'. Increasingly, tricks are replacing movement quality, technique and artistry in all styles of dance in studios, competitions and studio concerts. Many children are

PROBLEM TWO – The Alarming Rise in Injuries Among Dance Students

not learning to dance; they are merely learning how to be a 'performing monkey'. The inclusion of tricks such as knee drops, toe rolls, acrobatic flips, somersaults, no-handed cartwheels and contortion-like poses in jazz, contemporary, tap, and lyrical dances is extremely worrying and often nerve-wracking to watch as an adjudicator. This is because tricks are not dancing. They usually break up the flow of the dance and have no artistic merit or expression.

Dance should express the music and should have some meaning conveyed to the audience. Dance is art.

The other reason why tricks are so worrying is that quite often the child will fall or overbalance, and there is no acrobatics mat or any other safety measure onstage in most dance competitions where we are seeing acrobatic tricks in most forms of dance. There have been broken limbs and sprains and other injuries as a result. There is no need for these tricks, which are borrowed from gymnastics and contortion.

Tricks are not dance! Tricks are tricks!

The quest to win competitions and be 'Insta-famous' has also brought the marketing and availability of all sorts of apparatus to be used to stretch parts of the body, often in an uncontrolled and unsupervised manner. These devices can be bought online and used at home by children. They consist of such things as foot stretchers, stretching ladders, turning boards, and all sorts of similar devices that should never be used by dance students without supervision. They are dangerous because they can cause short- and long-term injuries.

Such apparatus as turning boards, yoga bands, TheraBands, exercise balls etc. are useful and non-damaging, if used correctly.

CHAPTER 3

Problem Three – The Global Sexualisation of Young Dance Students

There have been many articles written on this subject in recent years, especially on the sexualisation of young dancers in dance competitions.

Age-inappropriate costumes, music and choreography at competitions, concerts and other performances are of equally great concern worldwide. Increasing awareness and bringing the subject out into the open is enabling parents and families to ask questions and to say 'no' to inappropriateness. Much work is still to be done.

> Research supports that sexualised dance routines for pre-pubescent girls are age-inappropriate and potentially harmful and should therefore not be included in children's dance performances.
>
> (*Journal for Physical Sport Educators,* 29 August 2018)

Age-inappropriate choreography, costuming and music at dance eisteddfods (solos and groups) and at studio concerts are contributing to the global sexualisation of dance students. As an adjudicator of dance competitions, I have sometimes been aghast at what I have seen onstage. Though the majority of children at most eisteddfods are costumed properly, and absolutely beautifully, I have, on many occasions, found it difficult to believe the costumes some parents and teachers allow the young children to wear, not to mention the movements and music! Witnessing the embarrassment of the dads, brothers and other males in the audience from time to time who have left the auditorium or look away from the stage, I have, together with many colleagues, felt a responsibility to help change the culture. By drawing attention to the fact that to have our young girls seen in public in this way is wrong, we hope to improve the situation. Parents must be made aware of what's going on and not bury their heads in the sand.

> [...] "parts of the industry are overtly sexual, and marketing can be paedophilic," says Jemma Nicoll, dance school owner and Journalist in Sydney.

> (*Sydney Morning Herald*, 8 July 2015)

Age-Inappropriate Choreography

Karen Van Ulzen has had this to say about age-inappropriate choreography:

> I have long campaigned against the inappropriately sexual nature of much choreography for school kids. I can't believe the number of (mostly female) teachers who put their pupils on stage in skimpy outfits and have them strutting and posturing like mini adults. It's as if these teachers – and the parents who go along with it – have become so inured to the sexual nature of the dancing that they can't see how suggestive it is.

> Here is what one 'dance mum' commented on our own website: "What saddens me is that when I am attending dance eisteddfods with my daughter, who is 12, I have noticed that nothing has changed after the RG scandal. Costumes are still skimpy, dance moves are still inappropriate, crotches are being flashed towards the crowds and the whole time this is going on the parents are clapping loudly and cheering as though it's the best thing since Vegemite on toast and the judges have beaming smiles."

> The issue of offensive choreography has been of concern to some adjudicators and eisteddfod organisers. Some eisteddfod committees have taken a stand, by writing new rules forbidding offensive material.
>
> Karen Van Ulzen, *Dance Australia Magazine*
(23 September 2013)

Picture this: The curtain opens to reveal a dancer draped across a piano. Moving suggestively to the open bars of the music, she slides off the piano to show a costume that gives the illusion the wearer is naked except for a few strategically placed feathers and sequins. Attempting to belt out the song 'Roxie' from the musical *Chicago*, the choreography is provocative and risqué.

The audience applauds enthusiastically with loud wolf whistles and whooping—led by the girl's 'clappers club': her family and fellow students. I am adjudicating the ten-years-and- under section of musical theatre at an eisteddfod. I double check my glasses and look at the section title again as surely it must be a mistake and it is supposed to read at least sixteen years. But no—it is the ten-years-and-under section! Aghast, I write on the report sheet that 'in my opinion this routine is not suitable for this age group'. This is all I can do, and I feel angry, powerless and embarrassed as there are many men and a few boys in the audience (most of whom appear to be equally embarrassed). In my comments over the microphone I make reference to the fact that all dances must be age appropriate in costume, choreography and music. Afterwards I had several people, mostly dads and grandads, approach me with words of support for my comments as they all agreed!

An eight-year-old dressed in a skimpy costume, and full stage makeup, false eyelashes, fish-net tights, dancing to the lyrics of 'Who's That Sexy Thing?' is equally appalling, distressing and embarrassing to those watching, either as the adjudicator or a member of the mixed audience. No it's not cute—it's wrong!

PROBLEM THREE – *The Global Sexualisation of Young Dance Students*

The sexification of young dancers: Inside Australia's booming dance studio scene
[…] the show tracking the pre-pubescent stars of Abby Lee Miller's Pittsburgh USA dance studio. The show is a growing place of worship for thousands of aspiring Australian dancers, and the wallet swallowing the income of their parents who recently paid hundreds for their daughters to attend classes with Abby Lee, on March 13 at Bankstown Sports Club. Despite being known for its overtly sexual content and verbally abusive teaching tactics, *Dance Moms* fever has infected the country.'

(Jemma Nicoll, posted by *Collective Shout,*
Facebook, 28 April 2015)

In a world where we should be trying to protect our children from ever-increasing threats to their childhood and safety, I, as an adjudicator, am often horrified that parents and teachers put the children out onto the stage in front of a mixed audience to perform in the manner mentioned above. They show a total disregard for standards of any sort and I have quite often been embarrassed and felt sad for the children. I have sometimes even had to turn my eyes away from the stage. I recall one dancer in an upside-down position having no idea that her leotard was creeping up and exposing her in an almost obscene manner. In front of a mixed audience with dads, brothers, uncles, aunts, grandparents, this sort of thing is ghastly for the adjudicator as well as the audience, but what about the poor child? Once out on the stage it cannot be taken back and the child has been exploited in the most dreadful way.

It is not the child's fault. She was just doing as she was told and wearing what she was told to wear. Why does this sort of thing happen? Because the teacher has not advised the parent of a suitable costume and/or checked to see the student in the costume, or the parents have not checked who is teaching their child or what the child is learning or what they should be wearing, or the costume has not been danced in before the performance or designed properly for the stage. Whatever the reason, the child suffers dreadful humiliation.

'A paedophile's paradise' is how one elderly former teacher described the eisteddfods and that was more than fifteen years ago. She would turn in her grave if she could see what was going on now! Such Instagram hashtags as *#tilttuesday* have also brought the children into the view of the general public in the most exposed positions and rather skimpy clothing. As Instagram doesn't take down comments on these pictures, the sometimes-obscene comments are left there for the children to see. The fact is that these are children and these pictures of them in such positions with very little clothing on can be seen and shared by anyone. We strongly urge parents to monitor their children's social media accounts. Parents must realise that photos of their children do end up on the most horrendous and disturbing paedophilic porn websites. There is no point in parents burying their heads in the sand or turning a blind eye to this unpalatable fact: even though the idea of this type of exploitation is anathema to any decent person, the fact is that it is a reality in today's world.

At this point we cannot avoid mentioning the truly shocking and sordid story that hit the headlines in 2016 about the Sydney paedophile dance studio owner and teacher Grant Davies.

> **Former Sydney dance teacher Grant Davies jailed after sexually assaulting students**
> In September last year, the 42-year-old pleaded guilty to 28 charges relating to the grooming and ongoing sexual abuse of his students and producing child abuse material.
>
> The victims were aged between nine and 15 at the time of the offences, which occurred between 2001 and 2013.
>
> Davies, who ran the now-defunct RG Dance Studio in Chiswick, was arrested in May 2013 after his wife found inappropriate messages to a student on his phone.

In September last year, the 42-year-old pleaded guilty to 28 charges relating to the grooming and ongoing sexual abuse of his students and producing child abuse material.

On Friday, NSW District Court Judge Jennie Girdham sentenced Davies to a minimum of 18 and maximum of 24 years' jail.

In handing down her sentence, Judge Girdham said Davies' offending was "predatory and persistent".
"The offender abused a position of authority and trust," she said.

"No sentence could reflect the impact of these offences and the harm they have caused."

(*Sydney Morning Herald*, 21 Oct 2016)

CHAPTER 4

Problem Four – Unqualified, Inexperienced Teachers

Like any sporting or artistic pursuit, there is a huge range of coaches and teachers in dance, most with good intentions. It is the teachers who 'make' a dance studio. Without high-calibre, dedicated, trained, qualified and registered teachers, the studio is destined to fail in many ways. It will be a sham.

Unqualified, inexperienced teachers can do irreparable damage to children both physically and psychologically if they are left to teach whatever they like, make the class up as they go along, and include dangerous movements inspired by the 'Insta-culture'. A set syllabus needs to be followed and this means that the teacher needs to be qualified to teach that syllabus. Having a Certificate II, III, or IV in dance does not qualify a person to teach. Qualifications in recognised and renowned syllabi, together with teaching qualifications, are what is required for teaching. Additional qualifications such as university dance degrees, certificates and diplomas in dance teaching and management are also very useful.

All junior and student teachers should be mentored and supervised by a fully qualified and highly experienced teacher until they become fully qualified with genuine certification from esteemed national or international syllabi. According to Ausdance's *Code of Ethics for Dance Teachers*, 'Student teachers will be trained and supervised to ensure the school's teaching standards are maintained'.

PROBLEM FOUR – *Unqualified, Inexperienced Teachers*

Great care must be taken to teach children appropriate steps and movements for their age and development.

Teachers teach what they have learnt. Students who are trained by unqualified teachers whose teaching standards are not high inadvertently become unqualified teachers themselves and continue to teach the way they were taught because they don't know any better. Parents wouldn't send their daughters and sons to unqualified doctors or dentists, so why send them to unqualified teachers, especially when they are charging fees equal to the fees that fully qualified and experienced teachers are charging?

CHAPTER 5

Problem Five – Damaging Influences

It is widely thought that the biggest and most damaging influences have come from the USA with reality television shows such as *Dance Moms* and *So You Think You Can Dance*, the rise of social media platforms and the Instagram culture around the world. Many children become obsessed with being 'Insta-famous' and often post photos of themselves in extremely dangerous poses such as the tilt, scorpion, over-splits, needle, over-split leg mount, and other generally ugly contortion-like overstretched and hyperextended positions. With, or without their parents' knowledge, they post them on Instagram with hashtags such as *#tilttuesday*, hoping to get as many 'likes' as possible. They can (and do) sustain injuries as a consequence.

Dangerous forms of stretching have become a worldwide epidemic, but just because it is being done everywhere does not mean it's the right thing to do. Together with such movements as knee drops and toe rolls, and the desire for over-splits in leaps, and hyperextended legs, it is causing terrible and sometimes permanent damage to children. Teachers and parents must discourage this. Students are being pushed into performing choreography that is not age-appropriate and are not always being taught in the correct system of progressions and levels. This happens, for instance, when dance routines are 'recycled' and not choreographed specifically for the dance student or handed down from an older student to a younger one by an unqualified student teacher. It can also happen when visiting teachers take workshops for a wide age

PROBLEM FIVE – Damaging Influences

group. The age group might be seven to twelve years and the routine might suit the twelve-year-olds but not the seven-year-olds.

The responsibility rests with studio directors, teachers and parents to resist putting pressure on students to pursue these extreme movements, often in a quest to 'win' at any costs, or to become 'Insta-famous'. The risk of damaging children by performing dangerous and extreme movements and tricks in order to win competitions is unacceptable.

The *Dance Moms* series has created the idea that dance training is meant to be like the program. Full of brash, rude, disrespectful teachers, students and parents, it has given an unrealistic perception of what dance training is really like and is a misrepresentation of the majority of dance schools. In my opinion it is just a cheap, contrived load of rubbish. It appears to have been largely influenced by the pageant industry of the USA. It has gained popularity and a huge following, but colleagues agree it is cheap, trashy and damaging to the dance community at large. Dance has always been an art; however, now, largely because of these influences, it has widely become more like competitive sport, gymnastics, or contortion.

> [...] the show tracking the pre-pubescent stars of Abby Lee Miller's Pittsburgh USA dance studio. The show is a growing place of worship for thousands of aspiring Australian dancers, and the wallet swallowing the income of their parents who recently paid hundreds for their daughters to attend classes with Abby Lee, on March 13 at Bankstown Sports Club. Despite being known for its overtly sexual content and verbally abusive teaching tactics, *Dance Moms* fever has infected the country.
>
> (Jemma Nicoll, as published at Melinda Tankard Reist)

Along with the trashy culture and dangerous moves comes the overtraining of children, which is causing advanced injuries, age-inappropriate costumes, frequently age-inappropriate music and choreography, and overt sexualisation of children.

Another cause of these problems is lack of valid, expert and accessible information for parents. In a world where everyone can search everything on the internet, there has been a dire lack of guidance to help parents navigate the confusing, complicated and sometimes overwhelming dance industry of today. With information scattered over the internet on blogs, in online dance magazines and dance websites, colleagues agree that vital facts and guidance have not been easy for dance parents to find.

Heartbreakingly, many talented and gifted dance students fall by the wayside through incorrect training, advice and influences.

CHAPTER 6

Other Problems in the Booming Dance Industry

It appears that many teachers, who may be afraid of losing students to other studios, are bowing to pressure from parents and students who think it's 'normal' to be taught the dangerous moves and tricks they see on shows like *Dance Moms* and social media platforms such as Instagram and YouTube. Eventually, it is the children who pay the price. It is heartbreaking that the children can be the eventual victims of unsatisfactory situations, despite the well-meant efforts of parents.

Our children must always be treated with respect and not as dispensable performing ponies.

It is up to parents to be very careful when interviewing and choosing a dance teacher and studio. They must ensure their decision is based on solid research and hard facts. Parents need to know what's going on in dance studios and monitor closely what's being taught and who is teaching their children.

Parents are giving their treasured children over to dance studios and teachers for many hours per week, in good faith, blindly trusting in these studios while often knowing virtually nothing about who is teaching their children, or what they are being taught in the classes.

We do not understand why parents often appear to take advice about their child's dance education and pathways from people who have little or no knowledge, professional experience or real qualifications in the performing arts world. There isn't even the excuse of the fees being less at such studios than at reputable studios, because they are not; frequently, parents pay more.

Some parents who may be very busy with their lives fail to take a real, active interest and responsibility for their children's dance education and can only manage to pick up, drop off and turn up to see the annual concert. They have no idea what the child is doing or what is going on in the studio in general. This is unfortunate for the child. Parents must be proactive and ensure that the dancing lessons are not being used as a child-minding service after school until someone can pick up the child.

Once a top-quality studio is found, then the parents can be sure that their child is in safe hands and will be trained properly and safely. They can then step back and let the teacher do their job, keeping an eye on it all from a short distance.

There are the students and parents who will survive their dance training relatively unscathed physically, psychologically and financially. However, there are many who do not. These students and their families often fly under the radar and usually go away quietly—never ever setting foot inside a dance studio again. The damage has been done, and no-one is held accountable. No one talks about it and you won't see a post on Instagram about the poor child who's been seriously injured.

Not Everyone Can Be a Professional Dancer

Whilst we always endeavour to be encouraging to every dance student of every age, we must also be honest and realistic. The fact is that not everyone who wants to be a professional dancer or performer will be one. Why? For many reasons, the main one being that they do not have talent. Teachers cannot make a 'silk purse out of a sour's ear', as one of my colleagues put it. Nor can we put in what God's left out. But this does not stop some foolish or unscrupulous teachers gushing over a student and inflating the child's belief in their ability, which encourages the parents to sink more and more money into the dancing lessons.

The ethos and mantra that has been bandied about for several years now—that if you work as hard as you can, harder than everyone else, want it more, have more lessons than everyone else and put your whole heart and soul into it 24/7, you can be anything you want to be including a dancer—just isn't true!

It is unrealistic and unfair on the child to have them (and yourselves) believe this. It's equally true that not all children who dream of being an astronaut or a professional soccer player are going to have what it takes when they grow up, no matter how hard they try.

But every child can enjoy dancing lessons.

Their success should not be judged on how many competitions they win, who gets the top mark for their exam, or who is the best in the class. It should be a matter of celebrating the progress they are making and the enjoyment they are getting from attending dancing lessons.

As a teacher, we are only as good as our 'worst' student. And this is not meant in a derogatory way. You must understand that we very experienced and dedicated teachers get the most joy out of helping a student who has struggled for weeks to master a certain step or movement. The child keeps trying and one day, with guidance and encouragement from the teacher, the penny finally drops and the student and the teacher both have a real sense of achievement and joy. This may be the least-talented child in the class.

Every child deserves the attention, encouragement, correction and hard work of the teacher and every child should improve week by week. Some students overcome many things to dance in the end-of-year concert and this may be the highlight of their dancing years. I have had former students contact me, now grown up with families of their own, and tell me that the years they danced in my studio and took part in our annual performances were the best years of their lives. We never had bad injuries and in fact very few injuries at all.

Power and Profits

Dance studio advertising can sometimes give the impression of belonging to a cult-like ethos, and loyalty to the studio seems to be an expected prerequisite of membership. Isolated and often operating in converted warehouses, they can be seemingly oblivious to the outside world and the other commitments young dance students have, including school, other hobbies, and family. This can cause friction when the student is supposed to be at a dance rehearsal and a school commitment at the same time. Often the studio will put pressure on the child to prioritise dance. It can be quite stressful for the student, who can't be in two places at once nor please everyone.

In order for the whole studio to avoid being a complete shambles, a certain amount of control over the students and parents is necessary. This is the case where students need to be at classes, rehearsals, and performances, and the discipline of being on time and well prepared is necessary in dance. However, when those who are in positions of power seem to be put on pedestals through the branding and image-makers, parents and students become brainwashed. Some have a little too much control over the students' lives. They appear to be able to convince and control students, parents and teachers, who are often too afraid to question anything. They are too scared to leave the studio for fear of the repercussions. Parents soon begin to feel that the studio 'owns' their child and they must always do what the studio dictates—or suffer the consequences.

Sometimes families just don't know how to get themselves out of this increasingly familiar situation: They fear bullying from other parents and students and fear being accused of being disloyal by teachers/directors.

Before you know it, your child is dancing six days a week, is often getting injured and sick, and is always tired. You have no family time and can't take family holidays because of the extra rehearsals and competitions. The finances are suffering, the other children in the family are being neglected (or at least feeling neglected), and the marriage suffers. This story is common.

You may find that you are the target of some rather heavy-handed methods of persuasion. Don't be fooled into thinking that the studio has your child's interests at heart; rather, it is because classes need to be filled to cover costs. Parents may feel compelled to pay for their child to attend summer intensives, and other workshops taught by visiting teachers throughout the year, which are an additional cost on top of the regular term fees. To the young student dancer, these can be fun but will not have any bearing on them becoming a better dancer or a professional dancer later on. Similarly, there is little to be gained by being in a class of about a hundred students at a dance convention!

The subculture that has arisen and encompasses many dance studios has a dark side. Where young children are just wanting to enjoy learning to dance and wish to join one or two classes a week, there have been instances of some being belittled, bullied and ostracised for not taking up more classes, or attending more workshops and conventions. They are accused by the staff and students of not supporting the studio or of being disloyal.

Similarly, students mustn't be made to feel 'bad' for having to miss a competition because of illness. Children's health comes before all else and they should never be made feel guilty or suffer 'consequences' if they miss a performance or competition because of illness or injury.

Big Fish in Little Ponds

Colleagues agree it is not an ideal situation when students are 'big fish in little ponds'. They find themselves living and dancing in an insulated environment, especially if they also attend 'school' at their dance studio. They have little contact with the outside world and exist in their own bubble, with 'in-house' assessments and no exams or syllabus. This means the studio can 'pass' students onto the next level without them having reached any national or global standard.

Fierce competition between studios to gain more students is causing some studios to resort to unethical tactics and practices, including poaching students from other studios and relying heavily on 'winning' at any cost so they can further promote their studio on social media.

The need to fill up the classes with students to keep the fees coming in has led to another disturbing trend in some studios whereby the studio owners bend over backwards to keep the parents happy. Allowing the loudest, most persistent parents (or the ones paying the most fees) to call the shots is leading to some parents almost running the studios and to their children receiving favoured treatment.

CHAPTER 7

What is the Solution to These Problems?

Dance organisations have made efforts over the years to create national standards, regulations and licensing, which would be a major step forward. But so far their efforts have largely been in vain.

In the absence of formal controls, colleagues agree that the first step in solving these problems is educating and informing parents and students to be at least aware of what's right and wrong so that they are not blindly led up the garden path. At the back of this book there are links to various websites and blogs that provide further reading and information.

It may seem as though we are trying to 'shut the door after the horse has bolted'. Clearly, there is no single solution to fixing these problems that are affecting the children so negatively. Professional dance companies and contemporary choreography require the high extensions and flexible bodies, but children don't realise that the dancers that reach professional level are 'gifted' in physique and physiology. They are naturally flexible and 'turned out' and they have spent many years training carefully with esteemed teachers to build strength to control their flexibility. There needs to be more work on strengthening the body to gain more control and stability in the joints. The Australian Ballet is a leader in this concept, having several years ago introduced twenty-five calf rises on each leg at the end of the barre work instead of the dancers stretching. This has greatly reduced injuries in the dancers.

There are some wonderful Pilates/Gyrotonic-based training systems for ballet dancers, such as Marie Walton-Mahon's 'Progressing Ballet Technique', but we need to see these systems implemented for other styles of dance. We have started to see workshops in safe stretching for dance teachers that are run by physiotherapists (such as Lisa Howell, Perfect Form Physiotherapy/The Ballet Blog), and it is important for dance teachers in every genre to continue their professional development and keep up with the latest information. There has been a much-needed development of syllabus and certification qualifications for acrobatic teachers, as the incidence of dance students being injured from incorrectly executing acrobatic moves and being taught by unqualified teachers had been high. It's extremely important that acrobatics is taught correctly, and students must progress in stages—like building blocks—to avoid these injuries. Children mustn't try the acrobatic moves at home without being taught how to perform them properly by a certified teacher.

Duty of Care

Duty of care refers to the moral or legal obligation to ensure the safety and wellbeing of others. Professional dance teachers and studio owners/directors have a duty of care to all students.

Some teachers and studio owners can be at fault for bowing to pressure from parents and students and for allowing TV programs such as *Dance Moms* and the social media phenomenon to have undue influence on their studios and on their teaching. Although many senior and experienced teachers have an excellent knowledge of safe dance practice, there are others who do not.

To help curb this worldwide, unacceptable epidemic, **studio owners and teachers**—especially junior and student teachers—need to become better educated about what young children's bodies should and should not do. Knowledge of the various stages of children's and young adults' development is imperative to safe and positive dance training. Studios should have guidelines for teachers to follow and teachers should continue to attend professional development courses to keep up to date with the latest information.

Teachers need to be tuned into the warning signs that a student may be undergoing some difficulty with their training, nutrition and overall wellbeing.

Teachers and studio directors need to be able to take the initiative to suggest or refer the student on to further professional assistance should they become aware of any problem a student may be having.

Competition judges who reward physical extremes should focus instead on movement quality, vocabulary of steps, age-appropriate choreography, music and costume, technique, control and artistry, as dance medicine experts warn of increasing injuries in children.

Parents Must Be Proactive

Thorough research and investigation of every aspect of the dance studio must be done by parents before enrolling the child and a firm eye and ear must be kept on the student's progress over the ensuing years of training.

Parents must insist on talking to the particular teacher who will be teaching their child. Often an office staff member is assigned the job of meeting with the parent and enrolling the child. However, the office worker doesn't usually have a grasp on what all the individual teachers actually teach, especially if there is a large number of teachers on the staff. For instance, the office worker might know that the teacher is listed as 'Teacher Junior Jazz for seven-year-olds', but not know whether they teach stretching (or overstretching) or whether the teacher is in fact qualified, or whether or not they teach a syllabus.

Parents, just as much as studio owners, competition judges, and teachers, have a responsibility to ensure children are properly dressed, and dancing to age-appropriate music with age-appropriate, safe choreography.

Always remember that your child will be performing in front of a mixed audience. Children will usually do what they're told to do by a teacher and wear what they are told to wear. It is up to the parents to ensure their child is dressed modestly and with dignity and that the music and choreography reflect these high standards.

Always take some responsibility for checking what music is being used in classes, solo performances, and at studio concerts and competitions (eisteddfods). Check what costumes are going to be worn and ensure your child dances in their costume BEFORE going onstage to make sure it is appropriate for the movements being danced. Tights should be worn with all costumes. Make sure the movements and steps are not overtly sexualised and are age-appropriate.

The greater responsibility lies with the teacher, but it is your child. You are also responsible.

The sexualisation of children in dance has been researched by many experts and more information can be found online.

Too Much of a Good Thing

Dance can be a wonderful, rewarding part of a child's life, but it should not be their whole life. Balance is the key to success.

Dance is often too full-on these days and some children as young as seven or eight years go to dance lessons almost every day after school and Saturdays. Of course they love dancing, so they want to go as much as possible; however, many parents are allowing their children and dance teachers/studio owners to call the shots. Parents are being talked into allowing their children to enrol in more and more dance lessons and competitions. In many cases the parents don't seem to be able to say no to their children or to the teachers and consequently are paying exorbitant fees. Parents have contacted me, at their wits' end, increasingly stressed due to the 'over the top' amount of training and performing their child is doing and the money it's costing them, which often ends up in burnout for the child and an empty bank account for the parents.

If parents are not to be pawns in a game, they simply have to learn to say NO.

CHAPTER 8

How to Choose the Best Dance Studio and Teacher for Your Child

Dance teachers have a huge influence on the lives of young people. The ideal dance teacher must:

- love dance with a passion and have the utmost respect for the art of dance
- love teaching with equal passion and enthusiasm
- foster a love of dance and the performing arts
- teach correct technique and safe dance
- have extensive knowledge and qualifications in dance
- teach a recognised national or international syllabus and be a registered teacher
- have experience as a performer
- genuinely care about the wellbeing of each and every student
- inspire, motivate and encourage the students with positive reinforcement and constructive criticism given honestly and tactfully—neither gushing praise nor scathing criticism
- be honest and seek further advice if knowledge is insufficient
- be fair and kind
- respect every student, fellow teacher, and parent
- uphold high standards, ethics and integrity in every aspect of dance and conduct
- continue to learn and keep up with the latest information through professional development.

The Many Great Benefits of Learning to Dance

Children whose parents are able to send them to dancing lessons are lucky for many reasons.

We have already established that dance is a wonderful, fun hobby with many benefits for the child, provided highly qualified and experienced teachers are found. These benefits include improved health and fitness, friendships, enjoyment of movement and music, coordination, discipline, creativity, dressing up in costumes and makeup, and self-expression. In addition, dance students learn good habits such as commitment, punctuality, teamwork, consideration for others, respect for teachers and fellow students, manners, etiquette, self-esteem and confidence, poise, neat and tidy appearance, and many other life skills. An understanding of the art of dance and performing arts is another great benefit of learning to dance. Experts agree that dancing improves schoolwork and time management.

However, if the wrong studio is attended, then the results will be negative and detrimental. What could have been an ongoing, enjoyable hobby can end up being short-lived.

Dance parents should know that there are, and have always been, many excellent highly esteemed dance teachers whose expertise, knowledge, qualifications and experience are vast and whose dedication to the art and to their students is incredibly impressive and unquestionable. However, there have also always been a large number of 'bad' teachers. I know of one teacher who has never danced a step in her life, and so has not passed any exams or gained any qualifications, who nonetheless charges parents for teaching their children to dance—out of a book and very badly!

Teachers and studio owners have the power in their hands to do irreparable physical and psychological damage to children, including damage to body image leading to eating disorders. I have witnessed students who have been to dance classes for several years who have learnt absolutely nothing. Dance is not cheap, and costs increase as time goes on. Value for money and genuine expert tuition for their children is what parents should be aiming for.

The Importance of Technique

There is no shortcut to success in dance. It is vital that children attend a dance studio that teaches correct technique in all styles of dance through a recognised national or international syllabus.

Regardless of the reason for learning and paying for dance lessons, every child should be taught proper technique by a fully qualified teacher. This ensures value for money as well as gives you peace of mind that your child is being taught correctly and safely.

No matter what style or genre of dance is taught, correct technique and correct execution of steps and movements are of the utmost importance. The continuity of a recognised syllabus at each level of training ensures steady progress for the student. Correct technique and alignment are the best ways to prevent injuries and the best ways to ensure the dancer can dance for as long as they wish, either as a hobby or a career. Many a career has ended because of injury caused by years of incorrect technique. A dancer entering full-time training who has technical flaws is in danger of injury since the repetition of each step and movement increases with more hours of training. It is imperative that technique is taught correctly right from the beginning of the dance student's training. If an unqualified and unknowledgeable teacher is engaged, then the student will be at increased risk of injury, both short and long term, and will not have any chance of a professional career later on. Bad habits are sometimes impossible to correct but continuous repetition of movements executed correctly leads to success.

Learning a Nationally or Internationally Recognised Syllabus in Each Style of Dance

Teaching a syllabus helps dance organisations provide a support network and ensures continuous professional development for their teachers. Keeping up to date and maintaining knowledge and standards not only bring teachers benefits but also give them confidence that their students are being taught properly and safely. There are many syllabi for all styles of dance and information about these syllabi can be found on the internet.

Students and parents can be assured that by being taught a recognised syllabus, the student is learning in progressions appropriate to their age and development. As well as achieving the standard required each year, the student can be confident that they are being taught a syllabus that has been devised over time by experts in the field of dance and is safe for each age group.

Passing senior examinations in dance often gives the student credits towards their senior school certificate (in Australia). Whilst there are nationally recognised certificates, there are also internationally recognised organisations and qualification to be gained by studying a syllabus. Students who pass the advanced examinations in these types of syllabi can be assured of a strong dance education, which can lead to professional opportunities in dance and dance-teaching registration through international and national dance syllabus organisations.

There is quite a large number of dance organisations and syllabi in Australia and around the world—you will find some of them at the back of this book.

Looking for a Dance Studio

The most common way of looking for a suitable dance studio is on the internet. The next common way is asking around, or word of mouth. Both of these methods are risky and unreliable, especially if parents don't know what to look for.

Anyone can put anything on a website, Facebook and Instagram. As we all know, no-one checks the credibility of online content. What appears trustworthy is not always trustworthy. Just as there is fake news, there is also fake information in the dance industry.

Internet searches

Internet searches will come up with studios in your area or in your city and, of course, the studio that pays the most to Google will come up first on the list. This is not necessarily the best studio, though it may have a flashy website, a carefully designed social media presence, and expensive branding.

Beware the spin doctors

Just because the website and social media page look fabulous, don't assume that the reality of the dance studio will be the same. A flashy online presence often comes with a fair bit of spin and spin doctors are alive and well in the dance industry. Behind the razzle-dazzle there is sometimes little substance. There are studios that use taglines claiming to be 'the best' or 'the leading studio' in your city. Beware of such taglines, because the studio that is in fact 'the best' would never have to use this tagline in advertising—its reputation would speak for itself. Studios make many promises. Some may be genuine, but many are not. Businesses can use advertising to say anything they like to talk themselves up, and there is no governing body to check for false or misleading advertising.

Substance or spin

Do your research thoroughly to sort the substance from the spin. As more and more children are learning to dance than ever before, this huge market offers fantastic opportunities for clever businesspeople to build themselves a lucrative business. Clever businesspeople know all the tricks to suck customers in (in any business, not just dance). As in any business, some dance studio owners can appear to prioritise financial gain. Some studios dazzle potential customers with impressive, flashy and sometimes exaggerated 'bells and whistles' websites that can inadvertently or unscrupulously 'pull the wool over' naïve and unsuspecting parents' eyes.

Websites will list a number of teachers. However, these teachers may not all be regular teachers at that studio each week. Some studios list teachers that may only come in once a term, or once a year, or that no longer teach there. They may not update their website regularly. This is another factor to consider when doing your research on a dance studio.

You can check teachers' names and qualifications on the internet. Remember, if you are unable to find any information when 'googling' a teacher's or director's name, you can be quite sure there is none to be found.

If the seemingly impressive profile on the studio website 'talks up' their accolades and experience and you can find no proof of authenticity, then of course you would not send your child to that studio. For instance, if you google a teacher's name who claims to have had 'ten years' performance experience overseas' and find that nothing comes up in your search to validate this, you can bet that the performing experience claimed is fake.

So beware of fake biographies with exaggerated claims. Do your homework and google the names of all the staff and teachers to check their qualifications, credentials, certifications and experience.

If you can't find any verifying information, then the chances are there is nothing to find.

Similarly, a page on a website that has photos of past student success in obtaining jobs can be misleading. Studios post these to show a 'track record' so prospective students and parents can see they are successful in their training. However, we must ask the question: 'What constitutes a professional dancer or performer?'

Colleagues agree that a person who has only had a contract for a few months cannot be called a 'professional performer'. The same applies to a person who may have had some sporadic work as a back-up dancer for a visiting singer, for example. Such people are not professional performers.

A professional performer or dancer is one whose main job is to perform in professional shows and performances. So be aware of this when looking at studio websites. When you see the page of smiling faces claiming to be professional dancers/performers, you must research further.

Studios who run full-time courses (charging around $12,000 per year) need to show some success to gain credibility, and so may succumb to the temptation to 'gild the lily'.

Google reviews

Take no notice of Google reviews! These can be 'bought' by the business. Studios have their students, teachers, parents and so on give glowing Google reviews by the dozen. *These have no credibility.*

Often the studio that has the smallest advertisement or none at all is the best studio. They don't need to advertise because their high reputation is well known.

Advertising is big business on Facebook and Instagram, and social media experts are often hired by studios to create and manage ongoing advertising campaigns and alluring branding. But social media rarely gives a true and accurate portrayal of anything at all, so don't believe everything you hear, see or read. The happy smiles on the faces of the studio's success stories that are shown on Instagram and Facebook, often holding a trophy, are only a small percentage of the whole picture.

Websites and social media sites should never be relied on when choosing a dance studio—they are unregulated and can be misleading.

And the shelves full of plastic trophies in the studio's reception area may look impressive, but they do not mean it is a high-quality studio.

Word of mouth

Asking around at school or amongst friends is often misleading too. Parents don't generally appear to research dance studios properly and don't do their homework on finding all the information they need about the various studios available. Sending your child to dance lessons just because a friend from school 'likes' it, is not a good reason. Parents must not be sheep and just follow each other blindly. Rather, thorough research must be done, and decisions made based on facts.

Be aware, too, that often a clever business/studio owner will place the studio close to local schools, or even at a school, thereby ensuring a regular stream of students into the studio just because it's handy and convenient for parents and students.

So what should you do?

The only way to be sure of finding a high-quality studio with fully qualified teachers is to take the time to be smart and do your homework. Look for studios that employ teachers who are qualified to teach dance and who belong to a registered national or international organisation that offers a syllabus. This is the most important thing parents should do.

It is up to you, the parent, to do your homework thoroughly before paying out thousands of dollars on dance training. Parents and students with very little knowledge of the dance industry landscape are leaving themselves wide open to being exploited.

Remember:

- The studio owner/s are usually also the directors. Find out as much as you can about studio owners and each teacher's background, reputation, genuine qualifications and professional experience. Look for fully trained and registered teachers.
- Research any qualifications claimed.
- Send emails to established organisations listed at the back of this book and ask for advice.
- Find out exactly what is going to be taught to your child.
- Find out who, exactly, is going to be teaching your child.
- Ask many questions.

Types of Dance Studios

We have already established the importance of having qualified teachers for dance students who teach and are registered in a recognised syllabus no matter what the genre is.

There are many dance-teaching qualifications to look for when choosing a dancing teacher or checking the background of a teacher at a particular studio who is teaching your child. A teacher should have at least one of these qualifications, preferably together with professional experience as a performer and teacher. A teacher who is well qualified will usually have letters after their name.

Syllabi are available in all styles of dance. The Australian Teachers of Dancing even have a hip-hop syllabus. Their syllabi have been devised by highly qualified experts in their fields and are national or worldwide organisations. Studying a syllabus ensures that the student is being taught correct technique that is appropriate for the child's age and level of development. The students are assessed by a visiting and esteemed examiner before progressing to the next level.

Boutique studios

Boutique studies only teach one style—for instance, a Street Dance School, a Ballet Coaching Academy, a Tap Dance School. These types of schools are suitable for those students who wish to study one style of dance as the main focus. For instance, a Ballet Coaching Academy may also have one or two classes a week on proper Contemporary Dance technique. They usually have a limited number of students in each class and some accept students by audition only.

Beware of studios that use their senior students to teach classes.

Teaching is an art that is perfected over many years. Senior students are junior, trainee teachers and should never be teaching a class on their own. They should be supervised and mentored by a fully qualified teacher at all times until fully qualified. Junior and student teachers left alone to teach a class of children often find it a challenge to control the class, let alone teach. More often than not they will have the children just following along, copying the teacher. They learn virtually nothing, and it must be understood that just because someone is a very good dancer it does not mean that they will make a good teacher.

Damage can be done to children when learning from inexperienced and underqualified student teachers. The standards of technique in all dance styles are not met and this can lead to injuries. Children can pick up undesirable habits and unsatisfactory attitudes. Under the supervision of a qualified teacher these student teachers, over time, can flourish and develop into wonderful teachers, but they do need guidance for their first years and should be striving for much higher qualifications than a Certificate IV in Dance as this is NOT a teaching qualification. Student teachers who intend to make careers out of teaching dance should be studying for genuine teaching certification.

Many of the dance organisations listed at the back of this book offer certification courses in dance teaching in many different genres.

Unfortunately, many teachers, particularly student teachers, seem to be very concerned about being 'popular'. Flattering the students will make them popular, they think, so many teachers will 'butter the students up' with praise, so the children will 'like' them. Children are told they are fabulous, stunning, awesome, great, amazing stars etc. and this makes the teacher popular.

But this false praise is detrimental to the children and their parents because it gives them a false sense of the child's ability and potential. It also discourages the child from working to achieve a better level of technique and artistry. Why should they if they are already 'great'? It is misleading and damaging and inflates the child's ego—not to mention the parents'—and it is bad teaching practice.

There have been instances where the studio owner has asked all the children in the classes which teacher they like best and has then given that teacher more classes in the hope of increasing revenue for the studio. The teacher may not have been a good teacher but simply one that told everyone what they wanted to hear. In this way, the children retain their sloppy technique, bashing their way through the steps while believing they are 'stars'.

In a good studio with good teachers, the child and the teacher strive to achieve steps with correct technique and execution gradually. The teacher encourages the student honestly and gives praise when it has been earned.

The result is a great sense of achievement and satisfaction for both the teacher and the student. This occurs whether the student is the best or the worst in the class.

Part of the problem is junior/student teachers passing onto the younger children all the bad habits and bad training they have received. Junior teachers are cheaper to hire and if they've been trained at the studio they're now teaching for, they will have had virtually no experience outside of that studio and don't know any better. It's a matter of 'monkey see, monkey do'.

'Hamburger with the lot' studios

The rise in popularity of dance has brought a significant increase in the number of performing arts or theatrical studios. I call them 'hamburger with the lot' because they offer everything including the kitchen sink.

All styles of dance are available to all ages from babies to full-time courses. They operate out of large premises and contract a large number of teachers and a very large number of students are enrolled. Upwards of five-hundred students can be enrolled at this type of studio, which often focuses on team or troupe competitions.

'Hamburger with the lot' studios may try to lure the students to do more and more classes, competitions, workshops etc. (even though it is not beneficial to the child to do so and may put strain on family finances). In order to give the long-term students a 'job', they will often ask them to become 'teachers' when they have only a Certificate III or IV. It's all done in-house. This is another reason why a nationwide or worldwide syllabus must be undertaken so you know your child has reached the required standard and is being taught properly.

To become an accomplished dancer in any field a student needs a very high standard of technique. This is paramount. No amount of competitions, extra workshops, conventions etc. can replace solid class work.

Instead of taking on extra competition teams and so on, I would strongly recommend the student take private lessons from a teacher who is recognised and highly qualified and who teaches proper technique (not one who will spend the half hour teaching the child how to do a one-handed cartwheel, for example).

More is NOT better when you are booking your child into classes.

Many of these studios will wrap their classes into package deals that can sound good but, as with fast-food meal deals, often parents and students find themselves biting off a lot more than they can chew. As the hype gathers momentum, the temptation is to do more and more classes, and this is where many problems arise. With fast food you're unlikely to buy just a single burger for $2 when you can buy the burger, the chips and a small drink for $3. When buying a package deal of dance lessons, it is often similar. You might be persuaded to buy not just the jazz dance lesson for $140 a term, but a combination jazz and hip-hop deal for $190 a term. And so your expenses grow!

These studios often do not teach any syllabus. They allow the teachers (or to use the buzzword, 'trainers') to teach whatever they like to any age group. And this is partially why we are seeing eight-year-olds performing dances that should be danced by sixteen-year-olds, for instance. As a token of credibility, some studios will offer a syllabus for ballet, such as the Royal Academy of Dance syllabus, but often they do not timetable enough hours of ballet for the syllabus to be covered in the way it is intended.

Most studios do not offer syllabus classes in any genre and these studios should be avoided.

Some studios operate more like a 'dance club'. Praise seems to be a priority. Anything goes, and proper technique and general standards are not usually seen as important. Expectations of a high-quality dance education in these types of studios are not realistic and it's really just for fun.

When competition teams are emphasised by this type of studio, their success is based on winning. Of course, students are flattered by being chosen for the eisteddfod (competition) teams, which they often have to 'audition' for and of course pay extra for. It can be great fun to dance on the stage as a group and good experience working as a team and working towards performances with friends. But buying into the eisteddfod culture means a big commitment to even more rehearsals, costumes, and group performances and, of course, even more financial cost to the parents. It is a great revenue spinner for the studio. It is also a great advertising ploy for the studio.

The eisteddfod/competition groups, which for many studios is their main focus, are costly in many ways including the cost on families and family time.

For some students and their families, it is their dream come true to participate and they get a big thrill out of the whole experience. However, what starts out as a 'fun' experience can become quite the opposite as pressure from the studio to 'win' and to attend more and more rehearsals, not to mention travelling to eisteddfods every weekend, all take their toll on students and families. It can be a stressful experience. Attempting to pull out of an eisteddfod group can also be very difficult.

Parents need to find their voice to say 'no' to their children, the studio, and the teachers.

The Studio Floor

Dance studios must be equipped with a proper floor surface that ensures the safety of the students and teachers and minimises any risk of injury. Floors with slippery surfaces are dancers' worst enemy as they can lead to slips, falls and injuries.

Studios that teach many different styles of dance have the job of providing safe and suitable floors that cater for them all. Tarkett or vinyl flooring (otherwise known as Harlequin or Marley dance flooring) is recommended for all styles of dance except tap dance. There should be a separate studio just for tap. A safe and suitable floor surface is particularly important for ballet and pointe work. A slippery floor prevents the correct use of technique because the body is trying to keep the dancer on their feet. The dancer must be able to put certain pressure on the floor through the feet prior to alighting in allegro, for instance, and if the floor is slippery they will end up in a heap on the floor, instead of in the air. A safe floor is vitally important for proper use of the feet and technique in all steps, as well as pointe work and pas de deux for older students. Touring ballet and dance companies, for instance, travel with their own large Tarkett floor and lay it down on the stage of each new theatre they dance in.

The studio floor also needs to be 'sprung'. It is a requirement for a dancer that the floor provide cushioning so that when the dancer lands, the floor provides some shock absorption. Dancing on an unsprung floor that is hard and provides little or no shock absorption is dangerous because it causes injuries both short term and long term including irreversible damage to the whole body, legs, arms and feet. It is a requirement that the floor be 53 per cent shock-absorbent so that the floor absorbs 53 per cent of the shock and the dancer absorbs the remainder using good technique. It is unacceptable to lay vinyl or wood over concrete.

Look for a studio that has the following:

- **A safe environment.** There must not be any dangerous obstacles that may cause harm or injury to the students. This includes shelves or barres with sharp edges, furniture such as tables, chairs and any 'props' that might be in the studio.
- **Spacious and airy.** Packing too many students into a class is unhealthy. I have heard of teachers having to teach class in the doorway as they couldn't fit into the studio due to it being overcrowded! Ausdance gives the minimum space per student as six metres. The studio should also have good ventilation and, ideally, windows to allow in fresh air. This is important as the dance students are sweating, coughing and sometimes sneezing. The ideal temperature should be 20–21 degrees Celsius (Safeindance.com). Studios should have a fire-escape/earthquake plan, and drills should be carried out for all classes.
- **Viewing windows.** These are important so parents can observe their child in the class, as usually parents are not allowed into every lesson. Most studios have a 'parent week' at the end of each term when they can watch their children's classes, but it is very important that all classes can be observed at any time through this viewing window. This is so that you can keep an eye on your child's progress, and it is also important for child safety reasons.

Sound Levels in Dance Studios, at Workshops and Conventions

Dance schools that have more than one actual studio operating at the same time must have insulation to ensure the music from every studio cannot be heard all at the same time. Having the music blaring out from several studios at once is unacceptable. Each teacher will inevitably turn up their music so it can be heard by the children and then yell above the music. Then other teachers will turn up their music. The result is a dreadfully dire and impossible cacophony, the children learn nothing, and the lesson becomes a waste of time. This is particularly problematic when ballet music is battling against jazz, hip-hop or tap dance. Not to mention the damage being done to the hearing of the students and teachers.

Sound levels of 85–90 dB may cause irreversible cell damage. The higher the noise level is, the greater the injury. The consequences for hearing are also directly proportional to exposure time; thus, the longer this exposure is, the worse the damage is. This must not be allowed to happen—studios must be sound-proofed.

Competitions, conventions and workshops are also guilty of exposing everyone to too many decibels. There is no need for the music to raise the roof. It doesn't add anything to a performance, as it's the dancing and the dancers that must create the energy and not the volume of the music, which can, in fact, distract from a performance.

A dance school should also have a good communication system so that parents can be informed of any news, changes, and other information.

Your Child's Digital Image

Did you know that the main advertising strategy for studios is the success of their students at eisteddfods? Studios gain huge benefits by advertising their successful, winning students on Instagram and Facebook. Your children are advertising the studio for free!

Of course, the students (and parents) get a big kick out of seeing their photos on Instagram and Facebook, especially as there is usually a congratulatory spiel to accompany the photo, which makes the studio look really good too. The child, parents and teacher are happy—but what about the other children who can't afford private lessons for competitions? And are you happy to have your child's photo used in this way?

When you sign up to these studios you will also be asked to sign a release form agreeing to your child's image being used by the studio in whichever way they like. Of course you can choose not to sign the release form, but you will no doubt not have time to look at all the photos that are used to promote the studio and the studio doesn't have time to scrutinise every photo that's used on social media and other promotional material. So you can bet your child's image will appear somewhere regardless of whether or not you sign a release. Parents do not have any control these days of where exactly their child's image may end up.

How to Avoid Having the Wool Pulled Over Your Eyes

Buzzwords and advertising hooks

One of the most important things is that you find a studio that is run by true dance professionals who are honest and have integrity.

Dedicated, hardworking teachers and people who run dance studios need to make enough money to pay overheads and to make a living. They deserve every dollar they earn. However, a disturbing recent trend is the emergence online of business coaching companies. These people have set up websites and coaching for studio owners on how to funnel students in to cover costly overheads and increase profits. They use every trick in the book to lure more students into their studios and fill up their classes by using clever advertising ploys and 'hooks'. Such websites teach strategies for luring students into doing more and more classes, workshops and performance groups as a way of extracting more money out of them. They 'coach' on how to keep a steady stream of students coming into the studio, which can also steer them away from the genuinely top-class studios. This is fine as long as the advertising is authentic, but too often these strategies are not in the best interests of each individual student or their dance education.

You will recognise buzzwords, taglines and hooks being used on you if you keep your ears and eyes open. Studios often hire advertising gurus to set up their ad campaigns.

'Family' as an advertising hook

Many studios advertise themselves as being a 'family'. This tactic is a clever advertising hook to make people believe they are going to be part of a big, happy, loving family. It creates the illusion of a sense of belonging and security. As we all know, every family has its disfunctions and problems, so be wary of this strategy. Also, the 'family' tactic could fool students and parents into thinking that they owe undue loyalty to the studio.

The 'family' advertising tactic is well-known and not only used in dance. This extract is taken from Wikipedia:[3]

> Family is a popular symbol in commercial advertising that is commonly used to persuade audiences into consuming one's business' goods or services over a competitor. Consequently, the symbol of family as used in advertisements is functional – it both increases profits and builds a positive reputation among customers.
>
> The family symbol functions on three levels of persuasion: social, psychological, and personal.

Beware too much praise

In an age when we see children being awarded certificates for pretty much everything, including just turning up, many teachers are delivering the praise that the children and parents want to hear. Whereas in days gone by (many would call it the 'good old days'), praise was a rare commodity and students had to work extremely hard to earn a bit of praise from their teacher. It would normally

---

[3] https://en.wikipedia.org/wiki/Family_in_advertising

be in the form of encouragement where the teacher would say something like 'that was a little better'. When a teacher made such a comment the student would be on cloud nine because they would know they were making real progress. It would inspire them to keep working in the hope the teacher might notice some further improvement.

These days praise is often dished out constantly and comes in the form of the teacher exclaiming that the student is 'stunning', 'amazing', 'a star' etc. Believe me, if any teachers from my dance student days came out with such praise we would know that they had gone completely mad.

I often wonder if the teachers that are responsible for constantly over-praising the students actually have been trained as dance teachers. Dance students and children generally respect honesty in teachers and know they can trust a teacher who doesn't dish out 'BS' (for want of a better term). I myself tell the students straight out that I will always be honest with them. They know they won't be gushed over. I will tell them if what they just did was 'rubbish' and that I know they can do better. On the other hand, if I remark that they have improved, or performed a step or dance well, they know they must have danced extremely well. For students who have the potential to go onto careers in dance, it is important for them not to be over-praised as students. There is no over-praise in professional dance. There is very little praise at all!

As many studios are modelling their businesses on USA studios, remember that rent and other overheads are hugely expensive with very large premises and teaching staff. A certain number of students are required per class just to break even, and even more students are required to make a profit. Accordingly, studios are always looking for new ways to increase revenue. Teachers whose strategy is the frequent over-praising of their students, and telling the parents they have stunningly awesome, talented children, may be misleading them, but it does encourage the students to participate in more and more classes—and the studio makes more profit.

Tragically, once these students start auditioning in the 'real world' later on, they realise that they are in fact not 'stars', as they have been led to believe. This is a very damaging situation as they come down to earth with a very big 'thud', along with their parents who have paid out large amounts of money for many years of training.

As students are encouraged and lured into participating in all genres of dance, they are promised that they will become 'versatile' professional performers. The truth is, the vast majority will not become professional performers at all. Nonetheless, they can enjoy their dance journey, without taking every class that is offered, and avoid the damaging downside of dance.

Parents tend to succumb to unrealistic expectations of their children when unknowledgeable, inexperienced teachers get carried away and tell them their child is a lot more talented than the child actually is. Parents and students become deluded when promised opportunities and careers.

Over-praised students falsely believe their abilities and potential can lead them to great achievements in dance, when in many cases this is untrue. Once reality eventually catches up with them, it is heartbreaking for both the students and the parents.

It is advisable to seek second and third opinions if you are told your child is talented. Try to find an independent teacher who is highly experienced and knowledgeable, with professional performance experience, who can have a look at the child and assess their ability and talent.

No one amongst us can foresee the future and say with certainty that any child will or won't have a career in dance. However, there are many factors that make up a dancer in any style or genre.

Teachers with considerable knowledge can give you a fair assessment of whether the child is really talented or if you are just being led up the garden path by your teacher (who may be well intentioned but may not have extensive knowledge and experience beyond the doors of their own studio).

Your Checklist for Interviewing Prospective Studios and Teachers

Do not ever enrol your child online. You will know nothing about the studio, the teachers, or the premises etc., and you won't know if you've selected the correct class. Make sure you meet the owners of the studio and the teachers who will be teaching your child.

Know the answers to all of these questions before choosing a dance studio:

- Who owns the studio? What are their credentials, knowledge, qualifications and experience in dance and working with children?
- What are the aims, goals and objectives of the studio/dance school?
- Who will be teaching your child? What are their qualifications and experience?
- Do the teachers follow a recognised syllabus in each genre/style of dance your child is interested in? Find out what the syllabus is and research it.
- Do the teachers follow Safe Dance Procedures as outlined on the Ausdance website?
- Is any 'hands-on' forced stretching, overstretching or extreme stretching taught at the studio? If so, do not choose this studio.
- How are the students assessed? Internal assessment or examinations by a visiting examiner? Are examinations compulsory? What is the extra cost for examinations?
- Are the teachers and/or staff trained in first aid?
- Are there progressive classes for each age group from beginner to advanced level? You do not want your seven-year-old in a class with fourteen-year-olds, for instance.
- Do the teachers continue to take part in professional development?
- What is the Child Safety Policy and statement and how is it implemented?
- What is the Bullying Policy and how is it implemented?
- What is the Discipline Policy and how is it implemented?

- Is the studio based mainly on competitions? Find out what the extra cost is and what commitment it involves.
- Can you sign an agreement if you wish/or don't wish your child's image to be used by the studio in any way?
- What is the procedure for the annual concert?
- Does the studio allow you to enrol your child in just one or two classes per week or do you have to sign up for many classes?
- Are all cover teachers fully qualified and trained? (Damage has been done when the usual, qualified teacher is absent and a cover who is unqualified fills in.)
- What is the policy on missed classes due to illness or school commitments etc.? Is there a refund if the child pulls out mid-term? Is there a contract?
- Are you able to watch the trial classes? (Insist on this.)
- Are you able to watch all classes for children under five years? (Insist on this.)
- Does the studio insist on a high standard of uniform, hairstyle and general attire?
- How often are parents and family allowed to view classes?
- Does the studio have viewing windows or live video feeds?
- What are the fees and are there any extra costs?
- Is there an option for private lessons? What is the cost? (Parents must be able to watch private lessons or view them through a door or window. A child should never be alone in a studio with the teacher.)
- Are the floors sprung and non-slippery?
- How big are the studios and how many students are in each class?
- Is there air conditioning/heating?
- Is there good ventilation?
- Are there fire exits and fire drills?
- Are the noise levels safe and are the studios soundproofed?
- Is there adequate parking?
- How are the students 'managed' getting into the studio and class and being picked up afterwards?
- Are there adequate dressing rooms and toilet facilities with proper handwashing and hygiene?

- Who is your point of contact at the studio? (Usually, studios have a receptionist and some office staff.) How is information communicated to parents and students? Are there options for payment plans?

Do not be afraid to ask these questions and make sure you receive adequate answers so that you are satisfied your child will be in good and safe hands.

Mud Map of How Your Child's Classes Can Ideally Progress

Child	Lessons
3 – 5 yrs	1 x lesson per week
5 – 7 yrs	2 x lessons per week
7 – 9 yrs	3 x lessons per week
9 – 12 yrs	4 – 5 x lessons per week
12 – 15 yrs	5 – 7 x lessons per week
15 – 18 yrs	7 – 9 x lessons per week

This allows the children time to be children, to practise at home, manage school and homework, have family time, and have friends outside of dancing.

Please note: A student who studies Major Vocational Examinations in ballet in the Royal Academy of Dance Syllabus or other renowned ballet syllabi must ensure that the classes are ninety minutes in duration and not just one hour. The syllabus cannot be covered adequately otherwise.

Fees

The fees you are likely to pay vary depending on where you are and the studio you attend. However, below is an approximate guide to what you can expect to pay.

Lessons per week	Fee per term (10 weeks)
1	$120 – $180
2	$300 – $380
3	$450 – $520
6	$760 – $820
1 x 90-minute lesson	$250
Baby/toddler dance	$10 – $23 per week
Eisteddfod/competition groups	$150 – $200 per term
Eisteddfod groups classes	$180 – $220 per term
Private lessons 1 per week	$750 – $1100 per term
Some studios have a rate for unlimited classes	$600 – $1000
Some studios have a family pass*	$1500 – $1900

***Note:** The danger of family passes, and passes that allow unlimited classes for a child, is that there is a great temptation to do far too many classes for the good of the child.

Costume fees, examination fees, and extra rehearsals are extra, although some studios build the costume fee into the term fees. Performance fees and admin fees are extra.

Studios sometimes offer various 'package deals'. Be aware that these can be a false economy as you could end up actually spending more money than you need to.

CHAPTER 9

Starting Dance Classes

Before you start to look for a dance studio or teacher for your child you need to ask yourself a few questions as parents.

What Parents Should Ask Themselves
What results do I expect to receive for my child through dancing lessons?

Most parents want their children to enjoy dancing as a fun hobby and this should always be the reason. So few children will become professional dancers that this should never be the reason for commencing dancing lessons.

At what age should my child start dance classes?

Some parents think that starting dance lessons at a very young age gives them a head start. This is not the case with dance.

Baby and toddler dance

Alarm bells ring when we start to see advertisements for 'baby dance' classes from the age of six-months-old! Yes! When the babies can barely sit up! Exploitation of this nature, targeting babies and toddlers, is shameful.

How young is too young? Until approximately thirty years ago a child had to be at least five-years-old to attend a dancing class. Then the Royal Academy of Dance and other similar organisations began a 'Pre-Primary' ballet syllabus for four-year-olds.

Fellow teachers back then predicted that before too long there would be dancing classes for 'babies' and sure enough …

Following this there have been classes offered for younger and younger children. Running a dance studio has high overhead costs and offering baby dance lessons increases revenue for the studio. (Before long there will be dance lessons for newborn babies or even BEFORE they're born!)

Many baby and toddler classes are geared towards girls and teachers must always make sure that there are alternative steps that boys can enjoy equally. Some classes cater well for boys and others don't. For instance when the girls do their fairy runs from the corner, that's fine, but a lot of little boys (and girls) also like to do soldier marching, or to be a pirate, or a rugby player running and dodging with a pretend ball, and so on. We need to cater for boys as well as girls as we continue to encourage boys to dance. This should be happening from an early age. It can be rather off putting and engender a feeling of being the 'odd one out' if a solitary boy enters a room full of little girls in their fluffy pink 'tutus'. It would be a big step forward if some pre-school dance classes were just for boys; however, this is not very often financially viable.

Here are few things to look out for when finding a dance class for under-fives:

Children should get clearance from a doctor before starting dance lessons.

Be aware that in order to attend a dance class from around the age of three to four your child should be able to:

- Follow directions
- Keep quiet
- Pay attention
- Stand still
- Listen and focus
- Wait their turn
- Handle being corrected
- Be well mannered

Starting Dance Classes

Dance lessons for children under the age of four are just for fun and can certainly be an enjoyable outing for parents and children. But beware of any claims that the classes are anything more than a fun activity.

> *Alarm bells should ring if you see advertisements for 'baby dance classes' from the age of six-months-old! Yes! When the babies can barely sit up! Exploitation of this nature, targeting babies and toddlers is shameful.*

Who will be teaching my child?

What are their qualifications and experience? Even at a very young age, a child should be taught by a qualified teacher so you can be assured the teacher has knowledge of anatomy and physiology. Toddler dance lessons, even though they are dance play for fun, can successfully lead into the Pre-Primary type of syllabus training systems in ballet, tap and jazz when the child is in pre-school or grade 1. Learning from a qualified teacher will give the child a good introduction to dance and an opportunity to continue on and to progress up the levels of dance training. Often a child will be put off dance at an early age by going to classes that aren't following a syllabus of any sort and which are taught by someone who isn't really qualified and knowledgeable in teaching young children. Another point to remember is that a child who is made to perform moves and steps that are too advanced for their age and level will suffer injury and possible permanent damage.

Go through your checklist:

- Ideally, there should be a viewing window for parents. If there is no viewing window, then parents must be allowed to watch the class in the studio. Teachers will complain that having parents in the class distracts the children's attention. However, if the parents are 'trained' to stay quiet and still (i.e. off their phones and not walking in and out), then there should not be a problem. I taught many pre-school classes over the years and never had a problem with any parents or any children losing attention.

- There should not be more than ten children in a class under the age of five years.
- Make sure there is no 'escape route' especially for active and curious young boys who seem to be able to spot a way out of the studio and run very fast.
- Do all teachers, assistants, and staff have blue cards (working with children clearance)?
- MAKE SURE THE MUSIC IS NOT TOO LOUD! It is damaging for young children to be exposed to music that is too loud. Young children have sensitive ears. You can check the decibels with a smartphone app. If the decibels go beyond the 80-decibel range you need to let the teacher know, for the sake of your child's hearing, which once lost cannot be repaired. Even brief exposure to loud music greater than 80 decibels can cause permanent hearing damage to young children. The level should be kept below 70 decibels.
- The studio should be light and airy with good air conditioning for hot weather and sufficient heating for cold climates.
- There should be no obstacles, fittings or objects in the studio that could potentially cause injury or harm to very young children.
- If a child is not toilet trained and parents are not allowed into the studio or cannot view the class through a viewing window, is the teacher going to change the nappy (diaper), or is there an assistant teacher to do this? If so – who is the assistant? If the child needs to go to the toilet, are they confident enough to let the teacher know, and what is the procedure for someone to take the child to the toilet, or are they handed to the parent? All these questions must be asked.

Be realistic

It is not possible to teach children classical ballet or any type of technique in any style of dance until the child is at least five-years-old, and any studio that advertises it can 'teach' babies the basics of ballet and dance from 1.5 years of age are falsely advertising.

The children can run around pretending to be ballerinas, animals and act out little nursery rhymes and stories or wriggle about following the teacher and trying some jazz moves, but they can't be formally taught steps or technique. Experienced teachers agree that proper dance technique cannot begin to be taught until the child is at least five years of age and even then it is very basic. A lot of bad dance habits can be picked up if the child starts dance at a very young age. Fun classes are fine and should be looked on as 'dance play'.

Under the age of five years, you are paying for 'play time' for your child. Be aware that your child may well be bored with dance lessons by the time they are ready to go into a 'proper' dance class if they start too young.

They could well be 'over it' and tired of repeating the same sorts of activities for two or three years until they can start proper lessons.

There is a lot of repetition year after year for the children aged under five years and a limit to what a teacher can do with this age group. If the class is more for the parents to get enjoyment from seeing their child in the dance costume at a young age, that's fine, as long as you know what you are paying for.

Encourage but do not force

All children are different and a child who is confident at home may not yet be confident in a group. Children develop at different ages and go through various stages. So, although we must encourage children to participate in activities we think they will enjoy, at the end of the day we could be wrong. Maybe the child doesn't want to take part in a dance class. Sometimes a parent who missed out on learning to dance will want the opportunity for their daughter or son, but the child may not be suited to it. So never force the child who has tantrums and clearly doesn't want to participate. Depending on what you are looking for and your reasons for taking your child to a dance lesson at a very young age it might be better to save your money and let your child dress up at home. Put some dance music on and let your child use their own imagination, either on their own, with a parent/sibling, or with their friends. A lot of young children love to spend hours creating little concerts where they can include their little friends in presenting songs, dances etc. to music they choose dressed in costumes they've chosen out of the dress-up box. My children would even write little programs and put them up on the door advertising the date and time of the concert—like an invitation—and 'sell' tickets. As a three-year-old, my daughter (who grew up to become a professional ballet dancer overseas) even got together with her friend and put invitations in letterboxes in our neighbourhood (unbeknown to us) and one afternoon half the neighbourhood turned up at our house to see their concert, which we knew nothing about! It's great for their imaginations.

Most little children love music and will respond to it by dancing. They do not have to be in a formal structured class to enjoy dancing to music.

Just because a small child loves to dress up and dance around at home does not mean they will love or even enjoy the more formal 'class' environment at a dance studio. For a young child trying to follow the instructions of a teacher (often yelling above loud music) can be very stressful. For parents who might want to send their child to dancing lessons to calm them down, more often than not it will have the opposite effect at such a young age. Many children get very wound up with the loud music, the teacher's voice and the energy in the class from all the children running around, as often there are too many children packed into the room. This environment can cause some children to retreat into their shells and not wish to participate. There is plenty of information about children's physiological and cognitive development on the internet and in libraries.

A child can start recreational dance classes at any age. However, it is advisable to start ballet before the age of ten years due to the specific technical and physiological requirements of ballet training. Classes in jazz, tap, hip-hop and so on can be commenced at any age. The later the child starts dancing, the less chance they have of being in a class with children their own age. A child who starts dance lessons aged ten, for instance, needs to learn the basics of technique and may need to start with children who are younger than them. This can cause problems as the older child will be sure to be a source of curiosity for the younger children.

Boys often start later for various reasons but are quite often well-coordinated through sports that have also developed their strength, balance and so on. The world-famous Russian dancer Mikhail Baryshnikov commenced ballet aged eleven years. Quite often the parent will send the daughter to dance lessons and the brother, who gets dragged along to his sister's concerts, may find himself drawn to taking up dancing himself. Perhaps this is one of the reasons boys sometimes start their lessons later than girls. It is very important that boys do not get left in a class full of girls as they go through their dance training. They must train with other boys and preferably with male teachers as they get older. There are many female teachers who are very good teachers of boys, but there is no getting away from the fact that boys subconsciously pick up technical and artistic details that are taught specifically to girls if they are always in a class full of girls with a female teacher. As they move into teenage years, boys also love the physicality of working on *tours en l'air*, various grand allegros and *pas de deux* specific for boys and so on, for which it is important to have the expertise of a male teacher.

The ideal age for boys and girls to start dance lessons is between six and nine years in a proper syllabus, progressing up the levels. So, you see, there is no need to rush into dance lessons at a very early age.

Parents should know that it takes time and repetition for children to learn steps and movements with correct technique and thought and to absorb them into their memories and bodies. Too often we see steps and movements being performed with no intelligent thought behind them. Dance, if taught by experts, trains the mind as well as the body.

What style/genre of dance is best for my child?

Experts still recommend that children study ballet to begin with. Ballet gives the child a very good sense of their body placement, balance, self-control, coordination, musicality, to name a few benefits. Even if you have a child who seemingly can never keep still, ballet, if taught by an experienced and qualified teacher, will be of great benefit to the child.

If you insist on sending your child to jazz dance lessons aged as young as five years, then please find a studio that offers examinations and follows a set syllabus. Similarly, if you put your child into tap dancing at this age, make sure the studio is following a set syllabus and offers examinations.

In many studios nowadays examinations are optional, but all students should be following a set syllabus that has been written by experts in each style of dance. This ensures they are learning proper technique and are being taught correctly. They also will actually learn the steps and know them, and not just follow along.

The whole experience depends entirely on the teacher and the syllabus no matter what the classes are called.

Many genres of dance are offered at theatrical or performing arts studios: ballet, tap, jazz, modern, acrobatics, contemporary, lyrical, aerial, musical theatre, 'character dance', and hip-hop. Information on each style of dance follows.

Ballet. As stated above, it is best to start with ballet. Ballet provides a solid foundation for all other styles of dance. Ballet is a beautiful and intricate art. It originated in the Italian Renaissance and has been developed over several centuries. The first ballet school was founded in the late 1600s in Paris, France, and introduced in St Petersburg, Russia, by Empress Anna in 1738. There are several different ballet techniques and syllabi, but they are all based on the same principles; hence, a dancer can travel anywhere in the world and take part in a ballet class. Ballet terminology (the names of the steps) is always in French so can be understood in any country. Ballet is based on specific posture and the turn out of the legs from the hips. It is wonderful that such an 'old' art is being practised by so many young people all over the world. Ballet has many benefits. The person in the street who has had ballet training is easily spotted.

Jazz dance. Jazz dance comes from jazz music, which originated in America and has its roots in Africa. The various jazz styles change continually with the changing of popular music. Jazz dance (formerly sometimes known as modern dance) began to appear in dance studios and onstage thanks to choreographers such as Bob Fosse, Jack Cole and Max Mattox. The movements often have sensual qualities that focus on the isolation of the various body parts. For this reason, jazz dance is not an appropriate style for a young beginner dance student, but it is important for older students to study it if they wish to be versatile. Some studios do offer jazz dance from a very young age. If you start your child with jazz, please make sure the studio's teachers are teaching a proper syllabus. Find out what syllabus is being taught and research it. Otherwise age-inappropriate steps, movements and music can be a concern.

Broadway jazz. This is a type and style of jazz dance that you would see in a Broadway show. A good grasp of jazz needs to be mastered before attempting this style.

Commercial jazz. The sort of jazz dance you would see on cruise ships or among back-up dancers for singers.

Tap dance. Tap dance is where the dancer wears metal plates attached to the toe and heel of the shoes to make the 'beats', in time with the music, thus creating different rhythms. Like jazz dance, its origins are American, but its roots are in Ireland and the West Indies. Tap dance doesn't require any foundation in other styles and can be taken up at any age. Children often love the fun of making percussion sounds with their feet!

Contemporary dance. This is a genre of dance performance that developed during the mid-twentieth century and has since grown to become one of the dominant genres for formally trained dancers throughout the world. In terms of the focus of its technique, it tends to combine the strong but controlled legwork of ballet with modern dance that stresses the torso. It also employs the contract-release, floor work, fall and recovery, and improvisation characteristics of modern dance. Unpredictable changes in rhythm, speed, and direction are often used as well.

Dance studios often offer contemporary dance from a very young age. As it is not possible for the majority of children under the age of twelve (who may not be studying ballet as well) to grasp the concepts of real contemporary dance, most dance studios teach a form of commercial contemporary-lyrical dance. This is not based on the technical foundations and understanding required for contemporary dance, though it can be enjoyable for the students to dance and quite entertaining at dance eisteddfods and concerts.

Lyrical (slow modern). Formerly known as 'neo-classical' ballet, this style is based on ballet movements and steps. Flowing movements and interpretive qualities make for a graceful style of dance.

Acrobatics. The word acrobatics comes from Ancient Greek akrobateo, meaning 'walk on tiptoe, strut'. It is the performance of extraordinary human feats of balance, agility, and motor coordination. It can be found in many of the performing arts, sporting events, and martial arts. Acrobatic traditions are found also in many cultures. In the West, Minoan art from circa 2000 BC contains depictions of acrobatic feats on the backs of bulls, which may have been a religious ritual. In China, acrobatics have been a part of the culture since the Han Dynasty, over 2500 years ago. The acrobatics we see nowadays generally come from vaudeville.

Great care must be taken to make sure the acrobatics teacher is fully qualified and teaches a syllabus, so the levels of difficulty are taught in progression. Pleasingly, there are new acrobatics syllabus qualifications becoming available for teachers to study to make sure the students are being taught properly, which should limit the chance of injuries.

Aerial dance. Aerial modern dance is a subgenre of modern dance first recognised in the United States in the 1970s. The choreography incorporates an apparatus that is often attached to the ceiling, allowing performers to explore space in three dimensions. It is a potentially dangerous activity involving acrobatic work at various heights. The most common injuries are overuse injuries of shoulders and back, pulled muscles, bruises, fabric burns, and dizziness/nausea (from being upside-down or spinning). Children under the age of twelve should not attempt aerial classes. Strict safety measures and knowledgeable, fully qualified instructors must be in place.

Aerial arts are taken from the circus and are often included in cabaret and cruise-ship entertainment.

Character dance. Character dance is a stylised form of folk dancing and can be seen in many classical ballets. Classes are an important part of ballet training and improve the understanding of dance from other countries, as well as timing and rhythm. Girls wear character shoes with a low heel and a character skirt. Boys wear either boots or shoes.

Pas de deux (duo). A duo is a dance in any style performed by two people. A pas de deux is based on classical ballet and is danced by a male and a female. It often involves the boy 'lifting' the girl and teachers must be very knowledgeable in partnering so the dancers are not injured—particularly the boy. Pas de deux must not be attempted by young dance students and it mustn't be taught by anyone who doesn't really know what they're doing.

Hip-hop. Hip-hop, which originated among African Americans, Latino Americans and Caribbean Americans in New York, is a new form of dance that has come into the dance studio and onto the stage from street corners. Street dance styles are many and varied and the music is usually rap with a strong beat.

Pointe. Pointe is a technique where the ballet dancer stands on the tip of their toes in specially designed shoes. Not all students are suited to pointe work. It must never be attempted without having had several years of quality ballet training. A child should be at least twelve years of age and have built up the necessary skills and strength.

This summary of guidelines for pointe is taken from the IADMS (International Association of Dance Medicine and Science):

1. Not before age twelve years.
2. If the student is not anatomically sound (e.g., insufficient ankle and foot plantar flexion range of motion; poor lower extremity alignment), do not allow pointe work.
3. If she is not truly pre-professional, discourage pointe training.
4. If she has weak trunk and pelvic ('core') muscles or weak legs, delay pointe work (and consider implementing a strengthening program).
5. If the student is hypermobile in the feet and ankles, delay pointe work (and consider implementing a strengthening program).
6. If ballet classes are only once a week, discourage pointe training.
7. If ballet classes are twice a week, and none of the above applies, begin in the fourth year of training.
Further information: https://www.iadms.org/page/185

Musical theatre. Musical theatre is a genre of drama in which singing, acting and dancing play essential parts. Classes must contain these three elements.

Singing or vocal. Straight singing or vocal lessons are usually offered in performing arts schools. The teacher must be a qualified singing teacher, otherwise damage can be done to young voices.

Stretch and technique ('turns and leaps'). There should not be separate classes for stretching and technique. These should be combined into the scheduled classes for each style of dance beginning with a proper warm-up and followed by a proper cool-down. If a proper syllabus is followed, then all aspects of the training will be covered in a class and be appropriate for the age and stage of each group. Having a whole class of turns and leaps creates physical stress on certain parts of the body and a whole class of stretching is ridiculous and damaging, unless it's for senior students who are specifically studying Pilates or Gyrotonics.

Cabaret. A performance of music, singing and/or dancing, especially in a restaurant or bar. This style of dance is for senior students.

Song and dance. Similar to musical theatre classes but only concentrating on singing and dancing and not drama.

If you choose a dance studio that is based on a solid ballet syllabus and examinations, it usually also offers contemporary dance, and these two styles make up the basis of the training. Dance students ideally study ballet as it gives a solid platform and understanding to enable them to study other styles of dance successfully. It strengthens and enhances their technique and style. Ballet is the basis of all other styles and adds finesse, precision, strength, 'finish', physical and spatial awareness, control etc. If auditioning for a musical theatre show, for instance, a director will look at your CV to see what level of ballet has been attained. If no ballet has been studied (or very little), then you will be unlikely to get the job.

Of course, some specialist teachers only teach Highland or Irish dancing and sometimes you may find other styles in your city such as 'belly dancing', 'Spanish dancing' etc.

How many hours a week should my child spend at dancing lessons?

Consider family time and finances and the child's time commitment.

A young child should start with one dance lesson per week. It is very exciting for a little person to look forward to their dance lesson each week and to try out at home what they have learnt. It's important for parents to take an interest and make time to 'watch' and encourage as the child proudly shows off what they have learnt.

The lessons can be increased to two lessons per week after the first or second year.

If the child is enjoying the lessons, by the age of about eight years they should be grasping the technique quite well and showing improvement each year. Self-motivated practice at home to work on corrections that the teacher has given them through the week is very important to their progress. Nothing beats a special notebook, decorated by the child, for the writing down of these corrections. It doesn't mean the child has to fix every correction perfectly, but the teacher must see that they have improved by practising. This discipline will hold the child in good stead when moving into the senior years of dance and into a professional dance job, if your child is fortunate enough to secure one.

By the age of eight or nine years the child could take three lessons a week. These lessons could be in different styles, of say, two ballet lessons and one jazz or tap-dance class. As we have said, the child should always start with ballet and then they can pick up other styles much more easily. There is no real benefit in learning more than two styles at that age. The term 'triple threat' is bandied about these days. However, often when we pursue this too young, we begin to get the 'Jack/Jill of all trades, master of none' situation in many children who do a mish-mash of various styles at a young age. As an adjudicator, I notice the posture and ports de bras (the movements of the arms) to be the two biggest problems. A child who takes ballet and jazz, for instance, will usually hold their arms very stiffly and straight in their ballet dances as well as their jazz dances. This specific ballet posture is very difficult to achieve if the child is doing too much jazz dance, as is the turn out of the legs.

For a committed high school student who is progressing well, it is not unusual to spend three days after school and Saturdays. However, they must not let their schoolwork suffer. Directors of dance companies want to employ well-educated people and if moving into any other field of work later on, the student must achieve a high level of education. It only takes a split second to be injured and not be able to continue dancing.

Dance students who are hopeful of having a career in dance must always have a Plan B and must never neglect their schoolwork. Even the ones who do dance professionally will have to retire eventually and will need another career to carry on with for the rest of their lives (perhaps teaching or a dance-related career). Hence, these days, dancers in all sorts of dance companies also study university degrees and such like, so that when they finish dancing they have another career on tap.

Danger of Learning Too Many Styles Too Soon

Studio owners and teachers often talk parents into sending their children to as many classes and as many styles of dance as they can. Parents are told their children have to be versatile and be able to perform all genres of dance to be successful. A dancer aged eighteen auditioning for a job on a cruise ship needs to be reasonably versatile, but there is absolutely no need for a child to be learning three or four different styles. A dancer auditioning for a musical production needs to have been trained in dance as well as singing and acting. These genres can be added as the student grows up, depending on their commitment, aims and talent. Otherwise, they never have any time to practise, so they are repeating the same incorrect steps week after week, the teacher is repeating corrections that sometimes never get 'fixed', and schoolwork and other parts of their lives are neglected. Over the years, I have always insisted that a child who is lucky enough to be chosen to have a private lesson (on their own) for an hour or half an hour to learn a dance solo must have all corrections given to them fixed at the next lesson. If this does not happen, then the parents are paying again for the child to be taught exactly the same things as the previous week. It is a waste of the parents' money and the teacher's time. If the child has not fixed a certain correction, then the usual excuse is that they haven't had time to practise as they are at the studio every waking hour of almost every day. This is counter-productive.

There have been timetables in recent years where children aged between ten and fifteen years have been made to dance for twelve hours a day with only a twenty-minute or half-hour break at lunch time. This is ludicrous, and parents must not allow this to happen.

Often the teacher or studio owner will be unknowledgeable on the subject of child development, not realising that at this age there are specific training issues that need to be taken into consideration. Injuries and other health problems will be apparent if a child is made to dance for too many hours at this age and stage of development.

Dance students need time to rest and recover. Bodies and minds in general require time to repair and at least one day off per week is vital. Students who are mad keen on dancing will want to dance more and more, and it's up to their parents to rein them in and be sensible.

Dance teachers in studios who focus largely on competition teams will seek out talented students to be 'leaders' in their routines. This makes the teacher's job easier and if the talented child is quick to pick up choreography, then the other students can follow the talented child in the centre front. These students are often put into many competition routines as the studio is more likely to 'win' if their talented students are in the routine and in the front. The talented students tend to get used for this purpose. It is a big problem for many parents who need to learn to say 'no' to the teacher and 'no' to the student, who of course wants more than anything to be in every routine under the sun. There is a big price to pay with the higher risk of injury and the student burning out. There are many parents suffering financially, not to mention losing large amounts of family time.

Talented students have sometimes been 'made' to perform in a competition even though they have been sick or injured. This is clearly bordering on child abuse and it's up to the parents to find their voice and say 'NO' to the teacher, no matter what the consequences are. No child should be made feel they have to dance even if they are sick or injured. There are no prizes for these heroics, and you can bet your loyalty will have been forgotten by the next week.

If you are talked into enrolling your child in everything but the kitchen sink, do be vigilant. You may be convinced that you are doing the right thing but only time will tell. Remember, you can always change the number of hours or even change studios if needs be.

Manners and Behaviour

Over the years there have been many parents who believe that dancing lessons will help their child to behave better. It is not supposed to be the job of the dancing teacher to teach the children how to be polite, respectful and demonstrate good manners. It is the job of the parents to teach the children these habits before sending them to dancing lessons.

When I began teaching over thirty-five years ago, children were quiet unless spoken to, and they knew to put their hand up if they wished to speak to the teacher. They would say, 'Excuse me for interrupting the class' and if they were ever late for class (which was hardly ever the case) they knew to come to the teacher, apologise and give their reason. They wouldn't talk to each other at all during the class. They knew how to stand still and not fidget; they knew how to 'line up' and they listened carefully to the teacher. Increasingly, dance teachers have had to teach these things to the students before being able to teach dancing.

Parents also would NEVER talk if they were watching a class. I used to allow parents to all my classes, and they would sit on the bench seats at the side of the studio. Many parents would attend many classes. They would come in quietly and sit quietly. The children never lost their focus and it was wonderful. However, over recent years some parents seem to think they are at a football match and never stop talking. They think nothing of shouting out corrections to their children in the class or to talk on their phones and to each other. It's unbelievable that not only do we teachers often have to teach the children manners before we can teach them to dance, but we also have to train the parents! This is one of the reasons that many wonderful and experienced teachers are 'retiring' early these days.

Parents of children with behavioural issues may send their children to dancing lessons to help. Depending on the issue in question, there may be some success in helping the child. But this depends on the severity of the issue. Ballet, contemporary/lyrical dance would endeavour to calm the child down. However, some children with behavioural problems have so much energy to burn off that they seem to need a much faster style of dance such as jazz or hip-hop. It is a matter of trial and error to find what works.

Often a teacher who is very experienced and who gives the child attention and encouragement (and who doesn't tolerate bad manners or bad behaviour from any child at all) will help the child enormously.

Sometimes the child whose parents tell everyone (within earshot of the child) to expect bad behaviour from the child will set the child up to do exactly what's expected – behave badly! When an experienced and

Starting Dance Classes

well-qualified teacher sets out the rules and expectations of the class at the commencement of the year and insists on all children adhering to these expectations (with no exceptions and with consistency), then a great deal of progress can be made with each and every one of the children.

Many teachers work tirelessly to uphold high standards of manners and behaviour in their dance classes, insisting on the traditions and long-established etiquette. Their success has led to their students being very successful—not only in the dance world but in all manner of jobs and in life in general.

There is no point in sending your child to dancing lessons if they don't want to go. Do not use dancing lessons as a babysitting service. Children who have been 'made' to go into dance classes are not going to benefit, and neither are the other students in the class.

Of course, as parents we always encourage our children to 'stick at' something and finish off the term or finish off the year. It often takes a good year to become proficient enough to begin to really enjoy whatever it is that has been started. However, 'making' your child go to dance lessons when they obviously hate it is pointless. It might be a good idea to let the child have a break from it and perhaps when they are a bit older they may wish to have another try.

It is a good idea, though, to try to find out what it is that your child dislikes so much. In some cases the child won't actually know; they just don't like going. I have had quite a few parents speak to me about this problem and many of them have discovered that the child is 'noise sensitive'. Loud music and a teacher yelling at the children just to be heard can upset a child's nervous system and put them off dancing. Or it could be that they just didn't take to the style they were sent to. Dance styles differ, so it might be worth suggesting your child try out a different style of dance.

A word from the late Robert Young

Director and Choreographer the late Robert Young dedicated his life to the stage, producing musical theatre shows in Australia and New Zealand and frequently visiting New York to catch up with the latest shows and visit colleagues working 'off' Broadway. After directing the inaugural Arts Centre Gold Coast production of *Jesus Christ Superstar* in 1989, he directed and choreographed more than forty shows at the Centre, nurturing a talented and passionate music theatre community that exists to this day. Young also pioneered the Arts Centre's Summer School Program, mentoring young talent from across the Gold Coast and beyond in all aspects of musical theatre production. Many of Young's former students have gone on to become successful music theatre professionals and he continues to be remembered as an extremely generous and very honest theatre professional who always had the best interests of young people at heart. He was committed to nurturing and helping all talented performers to further their stage careers, asking nothing in return but their dedication and commitment.

Robert Young always insisted that if a dancer had a solid background in a ballet syllabus, they could turn their hand to anything, and have a much better chance of getting an audition and a job. He was known to say that if a dancer has learnt ballet to a high level, they have the discipline to turn up on time for rehearsals and not miss rehearsals. They will also be dressed properly with correct attire, be well prepared, know how to behave, and be respectful and courteous to staff and fellow dancers.

CHAPTER 10

Competitions and Eisteddfods

Christopher Powney, Artistic Director at The Royal Ballet School, has had this to say about ballet competitions:

> **Ballet competition culture: are we putting young dancers at risk?**
> A student's training is now so often being fast-tracked for these competitions in a way that I believe can be unhealthy. Ballet requires so much more than the physical and technical ability to execute a step or series of steps. I am not alone in feeling that some competitions foster a culture that fails to encourage the development of artists – where technique is emphasised over artistry and students seek to reach extremes before they have mastered the basics. We see audiences agog at the elaborate physical tricks on display. That audience should be looking for an expressive dancer trying to communicate emotion, dynamics, musicality, storytelling ability, alongside an accomplished, clean technique relative to their age. Isn't this what the art-form is truly about? This fast-tracking could potentially cause serious psychological and physical damage.
>
> (7 November 2018, https://www.royalballetschool.org.uk/2018/11/07/ballet-competition-culture-are-we-putting-young-dancers-at-risk/)

We have talked briefly about eisteddfods (competitions). They do have their place and many benefits and positive experiences may be derived by the students. In fact, a great deal of fun can be had, and friendships made. However, they must be kept in perspective.

Just because your child 'wins' first place in a competition, or has a room full of trophies, does not mean she or he has what it takes to become a professional dancer.

For the sake of the child, parents and teachers must not get carried away. Competing in a dance competition gives a valuable performing opportunity and sets a goal for the students to work towards. Of course, because dance is a performing art, an important aspect of a student's development is working on their stagecraft skills. They are an important learning experience and a student can ascertain how their ability stacks up compared with other dancers their own age. If all competitors performed the same dances it would be a better measuring stick of how one dancer compares to another. But a lot relies on the choreography and the skill of the teacher to showcase the strengths of the dancer and disguise the weaknesses. A teacher should not allow a student to perform a solo unless the child is technically sound, is committed to practising at home, and is confident enough to perform alone onstage. If the student is lacking in confidence it can be a daunting and even scary, overwhelming situation to be in. In this case it would be far more advisable for the student to participate in group dances or duos/trios until they gain more confidence.

Several years ago teachers discovered that increased revenue could be made by putting group teams and solo students into competitions. The studio charges extra fees for students to be part of the groups and extra payments are due for extra rehearsals and costumes. Parents must consider this before the child gets caught up in the hype and excitement around auditioning for these troupes. Many students also have multiple private lessons per week for several different genres, which can add up to a considerable amount a week on top of the term fees for classes.

Contrary to what many parents and students may be encouraged to believe, being in many eisteddfod teams does not mean the student will become a better dancer. If a career in dance is the ambition of the student, then they are far better off having extra lessons in correct technique (not turns, leaps and stretching!).

The 'Art' of Dance is Being Sacrificed

In the majority of eisteddfod teams, as both an adjudicator and an audience member, I have seen a few groups over the years that have been technically and artistically of a very high standard indeed. A few have even been so impressive that they have been of professional standard. I have witnessed absolutely brilliant choreography and performances.

However, a high percentage of eisteddfod solos and group dances nowadays have not been well thought out and the choreography is very poor. Because of the large number of solos and group dances that have to be churned out, the teachers appear to 'choreograph' them to a formula—that is, choose a piece of music, pick an opening few steps, then fill it in with tricks and combinations that are very similar to all the other dances, then add on an ending. We are sometimes left wondering if the music has even been listened to before adding the steps. Many of these 'routines' look like they belong in a circus or acrobatic show and have virtually no dance elements and no artistic or expressive purpose. Many of them lack any real dance technique or content. It is sometimes very difficult as an adjudicator to give the dancer a mark for 'musicality' when the steps don't even fit the music. The art of dance is being sacrificed when the choreography has little meaning. The product is not dance—it is sport.

Students who have been trained in these types of studios then become 'teachers' and carry on the teaching of these types of dances that are full of tricks and combinations that are set to a formula. They continue to churn out meaningless combinations that have no artistic merit. They are rewarded in many cases at certain competitions ahead of any piece of real choreography.

I have witnessed people in the audience at competitions being 'up in arms' when a piece of 'real choreography' has been placed ahead of a formula-style routine that's full of tricks. How little some people understand about art and technique!

Many studios treat eisteddfod teams like cheerleading or travelling sports teams. There is a great cost to parents and families with no real cash prizes to be gained. The expense of the ongoing rehearsals, costumes, travelling costs and sometimes accommodation expenses is a huge commitment. At least sports teams at a tournament will play several games and parents can watch their kids for several hours, but dance parents spend all that money and time to see their kids dance for just a few minutes.

I have witnessed children as young as four performing multiple solos in multiple styles. I have seen children under the age of six performing as many as seven solos and performing them all to an almost unbelievably high standard. I must state that it is quite disturbing to know how many hours of practice these children are subjected to and how much money the parents are paying the teacher. It is irresponsible of the teachers of these children to allow these children to be in such situations. There is no benefit in this at all. These children are merely 'performing ponies' and would be much better off being 'normal' children with dance as a part of their lives and not having dance as their whole lives.

> *Being a performing pony at a young age does not lead to a professional career and more often than not merely leads to burnout.*

Inexperienced adjudicators or adjudicators whose main aim is to be popular are at fault for rewarding dancers whose dances, costumes and/or choreography are not age-appropriate. They wrongly reward dancers who perform tricks (sometimes dangerous tricks) and who only perform steps and movements that are popular with audiences. These adjudicators also tend to write only glowing praise on report sheets and gush with compliments over the microphone. A shame for the competitors to be so disrespected that they can't be told the truth and be given the constructive criticism they deserve.

Adjudicators should (and many do) avoid rewarding extreme movements, tricks and inappropriateness. Studies have been done by intellectuals regarding competitive dance and it is of great concern to sport psychologists. However, there has been no study done on what motivates the parents, educators and children to want to compete in dance competitions. With the encouragement in the dance culture for children to compete and to spend endless hours at dancing lessons and rehearsals, there is no time for them to cross-train. Cross-training prevents overuse injuries, uneven strength between sides, and psychological burnout.[4]

As an adjudicator I have sometimes been left thinking that there will be a large number of dance students whose only chance of ever getting a job in dance will be as a pole dancer or stripper. Is this the sort of training parents really want for their children? Surely not!

Three Types of Dance Competition

Traditional eisteddfod

The well-established eisteddfods that have been running for many years are not-for-profit organisations and are structured in a proper way with a President, Secretary, Treasurer and Committee members, all hard-working volunteers. The people involved in these eisteddfod organisations often have a certain amount of knowledge in dance and the arts and raise money and sponsorships from local businesses as prizes for the competitors. They sometimes offer large scholarship prizes. Many students who have been awarded scholarships or prize money have been able to further their training. The intention of these eisteddfods is to give students a chance to perform onstage. The organisers are all wonderful people who give up their time freely.

The rules and regulations in these eisteddfods typically insist on high standards that must be adhered to. Their rules include insistence on the wearing of tights by all competitors in all sections. They do not tolerate expletives or inappropriate music or costumes. They have largely banned such movements as the tilt with the crotch to the audience, the shoulder stand split etc. These eisteddfods hire professional adjudicators, often from the Australian Dance Adjudicators (ADA) as these adjudicators have had to pass through screening and have reached the required standards and qualifications to adjudicate. The ADA has meetings regularly and oversees the training of new adjudicators. The competitors receive report sheets that will give

---

[4] Capranica, L & Millard-Stafford, ML 2011, Youth sport specialization: How to manage competition and training? International Journal *of* Sports Physiology & Performance, 6(4), 572–579.

positive comments as well as encourage the student to correct a step or work to improve an element of their performance. This is beneficial for the student, parents and teachers.

Competition franchises

There has been a growing number of competition franchises touring around in recent years, mostly from the USA, similar to the American Pageant model. These are money-making companies. They charge large entry fees to competitors (much larger than traditional eisteddfods) and offer very little in return in the way of prize money. In some, the overall champion will win a trip to the USA.

They seem to have many levels of 'winners' and will put an oversized pageant-style crown on the head of the overall winner—declaring them the best dancer ever!

These competitions typically reward *Dance Moms*-style choreography and have low standards in age-appropriate costuming and music, often rewarding dangerous moves and steps. Their comment sheets are usually full of gushing praise.

International competitions

Examples are the McDonalds Scholarships, Youth America Grand Prix, and Prix de Lausanne. These competitions are only for highly accomplished students with potential to have careers as classical and contemporary dancers. They are not for the faint-hearted, but the dancers have the opportunity to be awarded scholarships or apprenticeships to ballet and contemporary companies and sometimes a full contract, though this is rare.

Private/Individual Lessons

For a child to participate in dance competitions as a solo dancer, it is necessary to take private/individual lessons with a teacher in the genre in which they wish to dance. If a child is doing one classical ballet dance, for example, then they would need one half-hour lesson per week ($40 approx.). If more than one ballet dance is required, then the lesson would go for one hour ($80 approx.). Then, if the child is also dancing solos in the 'modern' genre such as jazz, lyrical, contemporary etc., another half to one-hour lesson per week is required ($80 approx.). Tap dance is usually separate, so add on a third lesson ($40–$80). Some teachers charge a fee for choreography and music ($100 per dance approx.). Others include it in the lesson price. So worst-case scenario would be a cost of $240 per week just for private lessons plus choreography/music fees. Then there's the cost of the costumes, and you would be looking at a total of at least $200 per costume (tutus much more), unless you are able to sew. Add on the cost of shoes and travel and factor in the term fees on top of that, plus any 'competitive teams' the child may be in, and you're looking at a huge cost. So it's best to do costings before getting involved in competitions.

Young dance students happily practicing safe stretching

One of the dangerous, popular moves causing serious injuries to dance students is known as the 'Scorpion'

Prolonged stretches can lead to loss of stability and serious injury and are not appropriate for dancers. (IADMS)

Gina-Marie Leathem showing correct technique and line, unforced and devoid of strain.

Ambitious parents and teachers must stop chasing instant success for the children

All children who learn dancing deserve a safe, happy dance education

Performing onstage is the highlight of the year for most dance students

Great care, knowledge and expertise ensures children do not dance en pointe before they are physically ready.

Noah and Juliette Krutzky. Baby dance classes are popular but are they a good idea for your child?

Dianne Leathem as the Sugar Plum Fairy and David Peake as the Prince in the 'Nutcracker", Southern Ballet Theatre circa 1982. Artistic Director Russell Kerr.

David Peake as the Nutcracker Prince and Dianne as the Sugar Plum Fairy.

Gina-Marie Leathem "Kitri Act 3, Don Quixote" Costumes do not have to be expensive to be effective

CHAPTER 11

Overtraining, Stress and Burnout

The idea that the more classes you do, the better dancer you will become is wrong. Quality, not quantity, is the key to success.

Overtraining often leads to an increase in injuries through overuse, stress and anxiety. If it continues for any length of time, overtraining can lead to burnout.

Many children and young adults give up dancing because of overtraining. The constant practising, classes, competitions and performances and the stress and pressure from continually trying to live up to the expectations of teachers and parents becomes too much. Students often want to step out of dance and into other interests.

Overtraining can also occur during a short period when there may be more rehearsals than usual for an upcoming performance. Sometimes these added rehearsals become so excessive they cause exhaustion as students try to keep up with demands. Often the students don't have enough energy to put into all their commitments and it can be overwhelming for them as their technique becomes sloppy due to fatigue, thereby making them more prone to injury.

Of course a certain amount of stress and performance anxiety is part and parcel of the life of a dancer, but we must be careful not to place too much stress on the shoulders of young dance students. They have to know it's all right to make mistakes and sometimes they will perform better than at other times no matter how much practice and rehearsal they have done.

'Too many classes and rehearsals, too many competitions, too many fees to pay and too much of everything' is a plaintive call I hear often from exasperated parents.

Cutting down on time spent in the studio leaves time for much-needed cross-training, practising at home, giving thought to what the students are actually learning and just resting or spending a bit of time with family and friends can preclude the onset of burnout.

The Misuse and Overuse of the Term 'Elite'

The word 'elite' is a much-overused term. Everything seems to be labelled 'elite' nowadays. What does it mean? According to the Cambridge Dictionary, the term 'elite' means 'the richest, most powerful, best educated, or best trained group in a society'. In the American Dictionary, it means 'those people or organisations that are considered the best or most powerful compared to others of a similar type'.

So you can see that when a studio advertises their 'elite' dance program it's one of those scenarios where the title of the program overstates the true calibre of those students who take part in it, as well as the actual program that's being taught.

I suppose what they mean is that they are learning and practising in the hope of one day being good enough to be called 'elite' and that they have the potential to become so.

Honestly, there is so much false advertising, misleading information, false promises and absolute nonsense being fed to unsuspecting dance parents and students. The worrying aspect is that in some cases the perpetrators of this false information appear to actually believe what they are saying.

There are dance studios advertising elite dance programs for students that sometimes also use the word 'artist', implying that either the students are already 'artists' or will be some day if they attend the extra program, which sometimes is only a few hours each week. No student of dance is an 'artist' and this sort of advertising is insulting to the true artists of dance—the accomplished professional performing artists.

An **elite dance program** should be one that is run by an 'elite' teacher: one who has had professional dance experience, has been trained by an elite vocational institution, and who holds letters after their names and has high qualifications from international and national organisations. If you can find a true elite dance-coaching program that is genuine, small-boutique style, then this is going to be extremely beneficial. You will know the teacher is not there just for profits and that true technique and excellent individual training will ensure your child is being taught safely, which will give them the best chance of pursuing a future career. This type of program works beautifully alongside the other lessons at the child's usual studio, or on its own.

So how are these 'elite' dance programs run? It seems to be that the teacher will choose the 'best' students with the most potential and talent and invite them to take part in extra lessons with other 'chosen' students. Some unethical teachers 'poach' students from other studios. The parents are asked to pay extra money for these lessons, which are sometimes labelled 'extension' programs. As far as I can tell, they are set up with the idea that the students will progress more quickly and be more focused as they will be together in the extra classes with other students who also wish to do well in dance. Quite often it appears that these 'elite' students can develop a rather high opinion of themselves as this system puts them above the 'other' dancers who must feel less worthy. It's not a desirable situation as many of these 'elite' students are quite young and the 'other' students who are left in the 'non-elite' classes can often develop into better dancers in the long run, devoid of the associated egos that are frequently evident in 'elite' students.

I have been told of certain teachers who offer 'elite' dance training for students as young as nine years of age.

At the bigger studios, it is expected that the parents will somehow persuade the school principal to let their child attend this 'elite' dance training for one day a week instead of going to school.

Let me tell you now—no child as young as that should ever be taken out of school to attend dancing lessons of any sort. A child of that age may show talent and potential but even the Vaganova Academy of Classical Ballet in Russia does not take children until they are ten years of age. Even then they are auditioned out of thousands of children every year and all the accepted children are truly exceptional and physically gifted for ballet.

Children must be allowed to be children. So please do not be flattered if your child's teacher tells you how talented your child is. It could well be the case that your child is talented, but if they are talented at age nine, they will still be talented at age sixteen.

The Misuse and Overuse of the Term 'Master Teacher'

Another term frequently bandied about, overused and misused is 'master teacher'. Many teachers who have had long careers in teaching and who have immense knowledge would be reluctant to call themselves master teachers and have nothing but disdain for any teacher that advertises themselves as one when they are not. This is misleading to the dance students and parents and we must call for integrity when advertising.

A genuine master teacher is a dance teacher who is highly qualified with vast knowledge and experience in teaching dance. It is not someone who might have appeared on a TV dance show or worked on a few short dance contracts. It has been brought to my attention recently that an eleven-year-old dance student in the USA was being hailed as a 'master teacher' giving classes at various workshops. It is utterly outrageous and extremely misleading for the students and their parents. True dance professionals are as disgusted as I am with this nonsense.

What's the Rush?

THERE IS NO RUSH, yet we find dance students these days, egged on by their parents, wanting to hurry to the finish line and turn into fully accomplished dancers before they are even teenagers.

An incontrovertible fact that must be considered is this: the bodies of children develop in their early teens. Some children who have suitable bodies to be trained towards careers in dance as children find they have changed into a physique that is no longer suitable. The opposite is also true and a child who might have shown little initial promise can blossom into a potential professional dancer. So great care must be taken not to earmark children for elite dance programs at a young age when so many factors play a part in their potential for future careers in dance.

It is true that some students benefit from 'elite' programs, but many others may find themselves biting off more than they can chew. Once again, for the young teenager overworking their bodies and minds can lead to stress, burnout, injury and over-tiredness.

> *If your child is invited into an 'elite' or 'extension' program, do think carefully before signing up and try to get a second opinion from an independent teacher or dance professional.*

Here's an example of there being no need to rush. My very dear friend, the late Beverly Millar, learnt dancing in Christchurch, New Zealand with Jennifer Cox, who became the mother of famous ballerina Julie Kent. Small world. Beverly told me the story of how Julie was 'spotted' by mega-famous Russian dancer Mikhail Baryshnikov when she was about 14 or 15 years old and was invited to move to New York to train. In her wisdom, and knowing how important family is, Jennifer—a ballet teacher herself—explained to Mr Baryshnikov that if Julie was so talented at 14 or 15, she would still be talented at 17 or 18, and so she waited to send her to New York. Julie had a long and outstanding career with American Ballet Theatre as Principal Dancer and is now Artistic Director of The Washington Ballet: https://www.washingtonballet.org/.

CHAPTER 12

Full-time Training

Full-time training should only be undertaken by very talented students who have the potential to be professional dancers/performers.

Careful consideration and research should be undertaken before sending your child to full-time training. Careful consideration must also be given to the age you will allow your child to undertake full-time training.

Many performing arts studios offer certificate courses such as Certificate II, III, IV and Diploma of Dance with the focus on commercial dance. Some offer a focus on classical ballet or contemporary. But parents and students often don't seem to know what they are getting themselves into or what they are going to be studying.

Some Concerns to Note

There are highly qualified studio owners who employ top teachers in their fields who hold auditions for these full-time courses and only take students who are talented. These studios also often offer scholarships. They have very high reputations in the dance world and do not hand out certificates if the students have not reached the required standards.

However, there are other studios owners who (needing all the fees they can get in order to pay their high overheads) take everyone who auditions regardless of whether they have talent. The assessments for these certificates are done in-house, which means the teachers and/or course director and/or studio owner will make up the assessment team.

They seem to pass all the students and send them onto the next year and the next level up, and then pass them for that certificate too, and so it goes on. Even the students who are not talented are encouraged to stay on for another year. Then they get spat out the other end of this 'factory', often having to pay off the years of fees owing and working whatever jobs they can get to pay back the debt.

Some Advice for Students Considering Full-Time Training

Why do you want to do this?

There must be a specific reason that you want to study dance every day, all day. Do you love dancing? Do you realise it's very hard work, tiring, exhausting and you have to sacrifice other parts of your life when you start dancing full time? When your friends are going out and on holidays, you will be dancing. Do you think you can sustain that sort of life? It costs a lot of money and the chances of getting a job at the end of it are very small indeed. If you want to dance full time because you think it will be fun, then you had better think again. Some of the time you will have fun, but most of the time it will not be fun.

Firstly, the decision has to be made by you, your family and your teachers as to what sort of full-time training you are suited to and what you have in mind.

You can try to get into a full-time vocational ballet school. Auditions are held for such establishments and it's best, of course, to study at a vocational school that's attached to a ballet company. It is very hard to be accepted into one of these full-time ballet schools as the competition is fierce and even if you're an exceptionally talented dancer, you still might not get in. It's preferable to be awarded a scholarship to attend; otherwise, you might just be making up the numbers. Full-time ballet schools are not for the timid. Competition between students is apparent and although you'll make friends, at the end of the day, you're competing for roles and attention from teachers and the director, and for jobs at the end of it. You have to absolutely love ballet and contemporary dance to follow this path.

You may have been told by teachers and others that you're very good at contemporary dance. You might have won a lot of competitions. But this doesn't mean you're suited to full-time training of any sort. Contemporary dance jobs are given to dancers with extensive classical ballet training to a very high level. So you can't get a job in a contemporary company having only studied contemporary dance. You must have been trained to a very advanced level in both classical ballet and contemporary dance. Also, there are few contemporary dance companies anywhere.

If you have a talent for musical theatre and go into a full-time course with the thought that maybe one day you will be able to perform in professional musicals, then you need to re-think. Do your research and you will find few opportunities for jobs in this field. Even overseas, jobs are rare and, of course, there are thousands trying to get into these shows. I have spoken to many full-time students who think they 'might like to go into musical theatre', not even realising that they must learn singing and acting as well as dancing to have a chance of finding work. It's a tough life. But for goodness sake do your research before forking out $12,000 a year for a course. You may be able to attain a Diploma in Musical Theatre and then go to university to become a high school teacher in drama.

What sort of job would you get now in commercial dance? Cruise ships? (Are cruise ships even a viable proposition in this COVID-19 age?) These can be a fun and cheap way to see the world, but perhaps a little risky in these uncertain times. Sporadic work as a back-up dancer for a band or singer? Sporadic work in cabaret somewhere? In some countries such as the USA, Germany and France, there is quite a lot of work in various types of cabaret. Perhaps you might try out for Disney or Universal in various countries. What job will you do between contracts? Whatever you do, don't give up your day job!

Unfortunately, jobs in dance companies are as rare as hen's teeth. It's no good for anyone to bury their heads in the sand and pretend that it's any different. But honesty is not always apparent when directors of full-time programs are trying to fill up the classes so they can cover costs and make a profit.

Less than 10 per cent of dancers actually get a job! We must now face the inevitable fact that due to the COVID-19 pandemic this number will be reduced to even less.

If you're lucky enough to get a professional job (and by that I mean a proper twelve-month contract), then it usually means living away from home. Away from family and friends. Of course, you'll make new friends, but there will be many challenges along the way.

Many full-time students are led to believe that by attending for three years they will obtain a Diploma in Dance, a Cert IV and a Cert III. You must realise that these certificates mean nothing when you go to an audition. The director will see how you dance/sing/act on the day at the audition. They don't care what certificates you have. If you have been trained 'full time' for several years but haven't reached a high enough standard (even though you have the certificates) you will not get a job.

Directors do care that the dancer has had ballet training to a high level. They don't need to see a certificate to know you have had this ballet training—they can see it in the way you dance, pick up choreography, and present yourself.

When you finish the three years of training, you will have paid $36,000. There are no student loans as there are for university studies, although in some states or cities there may be funding available. If you go to train in another city or country, then the cost is astronomical. Most dancers who study full time don't have the time or the energy to have a part-time job to help support themselves, so it's the parents and families who have to foot the bill. This can cause the student to feel obligated to succeed, and a lot of pressure as time goes on to give the expected return on the money and time invested in them. What happens if they don't get a job at the end of it?

It's fine to have a dream, but it's wise to have another potential career/job running parallel to the dance training: a Plan B.

I never thought this was necessary as my teachers would always say 'just dance', nothing else matters. This was very irresponsible. With the lack of jobs around and the chance of injury and just burning out, it is a MUST that dance students attain their school certificate and continue to study in other fields during their training and dancing years. Even professional dancers who are principals and soloists in top ballet companies study for university degrees while they're dancing. These days, ballet dancers need to be well educated and intelligent, and have a broad knowledge of all the arts. After their dance career finishes in their mid-thirties at the most, there is a lot of time left to 'do something else'. And not all will want to go into teaching.

Who should pursue full-time training?

Winning competitions and being the star at your studio do not mean you'll be suited to full-time training. Sometimes the dance student who's been quietly working away in the back row will be the one who is more suited.

There is a big problem for dance students who have been 'made a big deal of' by teachers, parents, and fellow students. The ones who have been told they are stunning, they're a star and amazing etc. will not be the ones who succeed in professional careers.

There are no stars in the proper full-time establishments, especially vocational ballet schools. Sadly, the ones who have been used to getting so much attention will fall by the wayside when they realise there is a big wide world out there and so many dancers who are equally as good, if not better, than they are.

Full-time training is just the beginning of a long hard journey, physically, mentally and financially.

Many attributes are required for any full-time training. It's just unbelievable that some commercial dance-based full-time courses seem to accept almost everyone who applies! This is unfair and misleading for those students who really don't have what it takes.

In addition to suitable physiological attributes, you need to have the right mindset and mentality to succeed at full-time training. You need to have artistry, energy, a strong work ethic, a 'never give up' attitude, a tough inner strength, and then you need to be able to 'perform' and connect with the audience.

No matter how much you love ballet, it's no good thinking you'll be a ballerina because you work hard and never give up—not if you've got the wrong body for it.

Similarly, if you have no rhythm or musicality there's no use thinking you'll ever get employed as a commercial dancer; or if you can't sing for nuts, there's no point attending full-time for three years thinking you might get a job in musical theatre one day if you try hard.

Do you get my point?

Anyone who doesn't tell the truth to a student at this level is failing as a teacher. Teachers must encourage and support students, but they must also be honest.

I'll give you an example. Toby was seventeen when he left school. He had been the star and made a big deal of at his high school dance program, so he thought he was pretty good. He actually had a good facility for dance, was enthusiastic, energetic, took his corrections and worked hard to get them right. He learnt a lot in the two years of full-time dance. However, Toby should never have been taken into the full-time course because he had left it too late to do any formal training. Had he started when he was younger, he might have been an excellent dancer. But by the age of seventeen there was just too much to catch up on and his body was already 'set'. He worked harder than everyone else, but all he got at the end of his course was a bill for $36,000 and a certificate. Three years later, he's still paying it off—working in a café.

Was it fair to put Toby into the full-time course? NO!

What should you train in?

Research all courses available to you. Get a second and third opinion on your talent and potential as a dancer. Don't just take one person's word for it (good or bad) and don't accept an offer of a place in a program because you didn't get anything else. Research and do your homework on all the teachers and guest teachers who will be teaching you. Check their qualifications and experience and by qualifications I don't mean a Cert IV. I mean real qualifications—letters after their names and genuine experience. If you see someone advertising that they've had ten years' experience performing overseas, find out what experience that is. It could be working in a bar! If you can't find anything on the internet, there probably isn't anything to find. Send them an email, or phone and ask. Attend classes and get a 'feel' for the studio and course.

Remember, you're interviewing the studio as much as they're interviewing you.

It astounds me to find people teaching full-time musical theatre courses who have NEVER been in a musical in their lives, and who have only a certificate to their name and no experience.

If you're paying $12,000 a year, you want the highest calibre of teachers possible.

Of course, if you are lucky enough to be accepted into a renowned vocational ballet school anywhere in the world you can be assured that all of the teachers will be first-class master teachers.

How are you going to pay for the course?

Usually, it's the parents who pay for the course. It's a lot of money. How are you going to pay them back? Are you going to work part time to help to pay, and, if so, how will this affect your attendance at the course? Will the director let you have time off classes to go to work? Will you be too tired to dance properly and get worn out trying to work as well?

When should you start full-time training?

Some students are starting full-time dance training as young as ten-years-old. This is totally unnecessary and quite ridiculous. These children are being cocooned in a dance studio all day and half the night, doing schoolwork and classes in an insular environment. Not to mention the fact that dancing for so many hours at that stage of a child's development and into their early teens is too much for their minds and bodies. We know that such world-famous establishments as the Vaganova Academy of Classical Ballet in St Petersburg, Russia, trains children from the age of ten years. However, it must be noted that these children are selected from thousands who audition each year. They have an exceptional aptitude and potential in all areas of dance, and they have their proper school lessons there as well. They are not dancing for hours and hours on end each day in all different styles of dance. Their training has been crafted over 400 years, whereas a lot of the full-time and part-time training towards various certificates in performing arts schools seems to have been devised by whoever is at the head of the studio and is a mixture of various styles and classes. They may not be constructed in progressions and can be haphazard. This can sometimes lead to an imbalance in the training as a whole.

A student should stay at school for as long as possible to get a well-rounded education. If they're lucky enough to go to somewhere like the Australian Ballet School they will be attending school lessons in conjunction with their ballet lessons from about the age of fourteen.

Sadly, there are situations where parents are being lured into sending their children from a very young age into full-time and part-time training. I've heard of studio directors telling parents with children as young as nine that the children must attend part-time ballet and take one day off school or they won't make it as a dancer. This is dishonest and absolutely ludicrous. After finishing Year 10, aged fourteen to fifteen years, a child can cope better with full-time training and schoolwork.

On the other hand if you're going to a course based on commercial dance, it's not necessary to go full time until you've finished school. There is nothing to be gained by doing any part-time course during the day and missing school, *except if you want the points from passing the course to go towards your school certificate.* Commercial dance jobs require the dancer to be eighteen anyway.

So think hard about what you want to do. Find out if you really have enough talent and potential. Have a definite goal in mind as to what you want to achieve and what you want the outcome to be. Research, research, research! Ask questions, get second and third opinions.

CHAPTER 13

Dance Jobs and Career Prospects

Many dance students think they would like to be a professional dancer or performer. But the fact is that not all dance students are suited to that life. There is a huge jump between the life of a student dancer and the life of a professional dancer or performer. Some dancers who do make it into a ballet or contemporary company are shocked to find that it's not glamorous, or not what they thought it would be, and that it's not the life for them after all. This can surprise all who have been involved in their years of training and dedication. It is a challenging way of life that requires courage. There are also many attributes that are required in order to 'make it' into the professional world and many variables that are out of the control of the dancer that can dictate whether or not they are successful in becoming a professional.

The number-one attribute a dancer needs in order to pursue a professional career is talent. Other attributes are a strong mind, tenacity, persistence, physical and mental stamina, a good brain, humility, dedication, endurance, confidence. The reality of being away from home, family and friends (sometimes on the other side of the world) brings significant challenges such as homesickness, loneliness, and a sense of unfamiliarity.

If the dancer is aspiring to become a professional ballet dancer, then they will also need the physique suitable for a career in ballet. Other avenues for careers in performing arts require specific talents and physical attributes, as well as the abovementioned qualities.

As a parent, bear in mind that the dream of a little girl to become a ballerina in a lovely tutu bears little resemblance to reality. Similarly, a young boy who aspires to a contemporary dance career may be creative and talented, but the reality of working in a company is that it is an exhausting 'job' and can be full of hurdles and disappointments along the way, as well as the positive and rewarding aspects.

Many young dance students have it drummed into them that if they want to dance, then they must put all their eggs in that basket, to the exclusion of everything else. This is ill-informed advice. All dance students should be encouraged to have a 'parallel career option' running alongside their dance training.

It should be remembered that the career of a dancer is quite short and in a ballet company a dancer cannot usually dance past their early thirties. There are some exceptions, depending partly on how the body is holding up.

Here are some of the dance jobs you might be considering as you weigh up your prospects for full-time training, your aims, ambitions and prospective outcomes (keep in mind that offers of contracts are generally for one year at the most):

- **Professional ballet/contemporary dancer in a company**
  A very small percentage of dance students become professionals and the percentage of ballet students who become professional ballet dancers is around 3 per cent at the most. There is little information to be found on statistics and research, but the number of students who make it into a ballet or contemporary company is miniscule.

- **Commercial dancer**
  The majority of students in Australasia who have trained in everything and are versatile seem to be happy these days to take a job on a cruise ship. In days gone by these jobs were snobbishly looked down on, and indeed in the USA a cruise ship job is usually something the dancers do when they are trying to find a better job (or are 'between' jobs). However, there have been a few fantastic performers who have successfully made a long career out of dancing/dance captaining/producing shows and travelling the world on these cruise lines. Some cruise lines are better to

work for than others, of course. The popularity of the cruise-ship option has allowed many performers around the world to have jobs when they would otherwise have found it very difficult to get work performing. However, with the global situation post-COVID-19, these jobs may well be fewer.

Other jobs for commercial dancers include being contracted for several months (sometimes yearly contracts) in variety shows in clubs in places like India, Turkey, Macau, Paris, Germany etc. Many dancers engage an agent in an effort to find work in TV commercials, music videos, back-up dancers for singers, concerts etc. This work is sporadic.

Dancers who meet the height requirements can audition for Moulin Rouge and similar shows. And there are several Event Companies in the major cities who employ performers to offer corporate entertainment, and themed shows for events. These are usually paid per show performed.

- **Musical theatre performer**
  In Australia and New Zealand these jobs are extremely difficult to secure. According to Sally Clark in her recent article in *Dance Australia* (issue 228), only 2–4 per cent of artists auditioning for a role in a musical theatre production are successful. These jobs are highly sought-after and few and far between. The amount of work available is very small as few musical theatre shows are produced and staged in Australasia. There are many more jobs for performers in the USA and the UK, but visas are difficult to obtain. Dreams of Broadway or the West End will probably remain dreams as visas are a problem and the competition for jobs there is astronomical with thousands of people vying for one job. To give a ballpark idea of the situation, if a dancer sends a video audition and CV to a ballet company, they can be one of up to 2000 dancers who are also sending video auditions. Out of that number, up to 500 might be chosen to travel to the actual audition. They are divided into several audition classes. Often at the auditions they have a 'cut' after the barre, then one after adagio, another after allegro. Then you might get called back to

dance again later on in the day. In the meantime they will repeat the process for all the other audition classes, ending up with perhaps 20–30 'called back' dancers; these dancers are asked to perform perhaps pas de deux and contemporary or a classical solo. Out of those, perhaps one contract is offered, and sometimes none. This scenario is common in auditions for other types of jobs in the performing arts.

The other method of auditioning is by attending a company class with the dancers of the company, if lucky enough to be invited. Many dancers will travel around Europe and the UK when the auditions are being held, having been 'invited' to attend. It is very costly, and travel and accommodation expenses quickly mount up. It is also daunting and deflating for the dancers who may have travelled a long way just to be 'cut' after the barre (or during), for instance, and mentally taxing for all the brave dancers. Often they are told they will 'hear' from the director in the months to follow, but no correspondence ever arrives. The same is true for any performer who puts themselves in this situation of auditioning—hoping, working hard, being disappointed, trying to keep positive, trying not to throw in the towel and give up on the dream. For those lucky ones that we hear about who secure contracts, their dream does come true. But for an enormous number of performers, it does not. They may sustain injury, or at the end of the day, just not be good enough.

When reality hits, they need another 'career' or interest to 'fall back on'. I believe it is the duty of teachers and other dance professionals not to overstate a dance student's talent, to be realistic and 'real' with regards to possible career paths. Now more than ever, as dance jobs have dwindled, and it's become increasingly harder to find work, teachers should guide the students into vocational full-time schools that feed into dance companies, or solid, potential commercial work. It must be remembered that approximately half of dancers earn less than $10,000 a year as freelancers in the industry. The increased number of graduates of full-time courses and the reality of fewer available jobs calls for a reality check, realistic goal setting, and honest—not overstated—appraisals of the student's talents and potential. I would encourage students (now more than ever) to get a second and third opinion.

- **Choreographer**
  A student cannot really train to become a choreographer. Though the fundamentals of choreography can be taught, anyone who becomes a working choreographer who makes a living from this art is a person who has a gift or natural talent. Dancers and dance teachers can arrange steps to music. That is not the same as being a true choreographer of original works.

- **Director**
  A director of a dance company or show is a person who has had vast experience in dance and who is highly esteemed in the dance world. They must also have a good head for business.

- **Teacher in a high school or college**
  This job requires that the student obtain a degree in dance from a university as well as a teaching degree.

- **Teacher in a privately-run dance studio**
  While no qualifications or licences are required to teach dancing in a privately-run studio, one would hope that the teacher has taken it upon themselves to obtain solid certification and training from a renowned and respected worldwide (or at least national) organisation. They should be thoroughly trained and experienced in teaching children.

- **Owner of a privately-run dance studio**
  Officially, no qualifications or licences are required to run a dance studio. However, one would hope that the owner would have some knowledge of dance and performing arts and the teaching of it. And, of course, some idea of how to run a business.

CHAPTER 14

Home-schooling

Some teachers of talented dance students want them to take on full-time training from a young age of around fourteen years, and this requires that they do home-schooling. This is a big responsibility for the parents and is very time consuming. It is not advisable unless you have had a second or third opinion on your child's ability and potential that backs up the teacher's opinion. This pathway is only advisable if your child is truly gifted and talented enough to pursue a career in dance. Home-schooling a child or taking on full-time training prior to finishing Year 10 at school is very ill-advised.

If you are intending to home-school your child, please be aware that it is a challenging undertaking. Your child will be spending most of most days at the dance studio and the idea of having to do schoolwork in many cases will not be appealing. Also, the child will be tired and needing to rest. The demands of the studio and dance teachers will often mean there is no time for online face-to-face tutoring, so the parent is 'it' as far as playing the role of teacher and the one whose job it is to actually get the child to do the schoolwork. Some children are keen to keep up with their schoolwork and if your child is one of these it will make your job of home-schooling much easier.

You will find that the 'hamburger with the lot' (performing arts) studios sometimes offer 'home-schooling' at the studio once students reach high school age. Students of various ages will sit in a room together to do their schoolwork during the day and will sometimes be provided with a supervisor. This is very costly as not only do parents

Home-schooling

have to pay the dance studio for the 'home-schooling', they also have to pay the online organisation through which the home-schooling is done. At 3 pm or so the students will go into the studio for their lessons. So they seldom mix with kids outside of the dance studio, living their lives in an insulated environment.

This does not create a well-rounded person and if eventually fortunate enough to work in a ballet company, for instance, this isolated way of growing up can often prevent them from blending in and mixing well with other dancers. Children who have been the 'star' of their studio or, in other words, a big fish in a small pond, unfortunately can tend to have an air of superiority, which artistic directors of companies loathe and will not tolerate. Dancers need to have a well-rounded education and mix with a wide range of people and show humility.

CHAPTER 15

Summer Programs

As occurs continuously in the world of the arts, dance companies and dance schools are always trying to find ways to increase revenue. Imagine their delight when a new phenomenon—the summer dance program—appeared on the horizon. Perhaps the idea was sparked by the success of the summer camps in the USA? What a fantastic idea and a great way to increase revenue during the dance studio holiday breaks.

Now there are summer programs all over the world giving dance students a fantastic choice and opportunity—at a cost to the parents of course.

Esteemed dance establishments audition students for their summer programs and some give selected students scholarships to attend. Unfortunately, travel and accommodation expenses are not covered and it's a sad fact that only students of more wealthy parents can afford to attend, unless the student can source funding through other means.

As well as the renowned dance schools, we are seeing almost every dance studio offering summer programs. Most of these are held before the students return from summer holidays and some are held during the winter holiday break. Of course, keen students want to attend these programs with their friends and it's usually a greatly anticipated event amongst the young students.

Parents are once again digging deep into their pockets to fund the summer programs, after having had Christmas and the family summer holiday to pay for. Not to mention the upcoming dance term fees.

So what benefit are these summer programs to the dance students?

If a student is genuinely talented and shows potential, they may be lucky enough to be accepted into a renowned summer dance program, usually in another city or another country. If the student's parents can afford to send the child, then there are great benefits for this student. Not only will they have their eyes opened to a big wide world of dance, with dozens and dozens of equally talented dance students, but they will realise how hard they must work. It shows them that they are not a big fish in a little pond, but that the pond is actually a vast sea and they are just one small fish in this sea. This is beneficial for the student, giving them a healthier perspective on what's required to 'make it' as a dancer.

Aside from this, the student will have the great privilege of being taught by true master teachers, often the best in the world. Learning from such highly esteemed teachers and choreographers is gold. And whether the student goes onto dance or becomes a teacher, such valuable knowledge gained will stand them in good stead. The student will make friends from other parts of the world at these international summer programs and find out so much more about the art of dance than they would have otherwise. They will see how hard other dancers work and how dedicated and talented they are and will learn from them as well as learning from the teachers. It's an inspiring environment for a young student and the value of this type of program cannot be overestimated.

My daughter, Gina-Marie Leathem, was one of the lucky ones chosen to participate in the American Ballet Theatre Summer Intensive in New York City. She was invited after a successful trip to New York for the YAGP (Youth America Grands Prix). We were not a wealthy family at all, and we sourced financial help from philanthropic and arts foundations, which was a huge job. But we got her there and having had a fantastic six weeks in New York at the Summer Intensive, she was named a National Training Scholar and invited back the following year on scholarship. She received scholarships for the next four years; however, we still had to find the funds for the airfares and accommodation. Eventually, she was invited to join the Jacqueline Kennedy Onassis School at the American Ballet Theatre Pre-Professional program (please note that even this esteemed program was not an all-day training program; in fact, classes only started for this level mid-afternoon). It was a huge cost and because of her age she had to be chaperoned in her accommodation in New York, but the experience was truly amazing and well worth every cent. The performances at the end of the six weeks were events not to be missed and seeing such young talent together onstage was astounding. It gives the students an idea of what a professional dance career might look like, but it is not for the faint-hearted. Six-week programs are exhausting, exhilarating and totally awe inspiring, especially in such a city as New York.

My point is that if you can find the funds and your child definitely has true talent, then it's an opportunity not to be missed.

On the other end of the scale, there are the local studios who have summer courses that can also be worthwhile for getting students back into shape and some sort of technical level before starting the new term. In a lot of cases, the students have their usual teachers taking the courses, and most of the time the studio engages some guest teachers to add interest. I don't consider these types of courses to be necessary, but if you can afford them, then by all means go for it. It's a great way to support the studio and see friends and teachers before the term begins. Some courses are run during the midyear break, usually before examinations are held. Various recognised training systems who hold exams have a set syllabus that is followed, and teachers and examiners often hold workshops and programs to brush up the work prior to the students sitting their examinations. These are worthwhile and beneficial for the students, as they help get the finer points and details under control and give them a bit of extra confidence before the often-nerve-wracking experience of participating in an exam.

Summer programs have age specifications and some establishments will have junior, intermediate and advanced levels. Some even add extra levels like, sub-junior, sub-intermediate, sub-advanced etc. Other programs cater for students over the age of eleven or twelve years.

CHAPTER 16

Examinations

Children can start sitting dance exams at a young age. It's up to parents, children and their teachers to decide what age is best to start.

While the word 'examination' can strike fear into the heart of many students—the very thought of being 'examined' can be daunting—following a syllabus and entering for examinations are highly recommended and the benefits cannot be underestimated

And exams are not nearly as scary as they used to be; examiners tend to be less harsh now.

When I was a student, the examinations were a big deal. They each required two solid years of work and to even pass an exam in those days was a massive achievement. Most students expected to fail and so no-one worried about it. Everyone worked hard and achieved as high a standard as they possibly could and no-one thought anything much of 'failing'. Many students would try again and many would realise quite rightly that they were not cut out for careers in dance after all. No-one was fed gushing and false praise because there was much more honesty back then. Now the poor kids, when they get knocked back after fronting up for auditions in their vulnerable teens, get a massive shock, along with their perplexed parents, at the realisation that they don't actually have the talent after all.

These days the word 'fail' is not even used. Instead of seeing 'pass' or 'fail' on the report sheet, the students see words like 'successful' and 'unsuccessful', designed to soften the blow. Few children 'fail' exams now with examiners trying to find ways to pass every student if they possibly can. The better students will receive higher marks and the students who danced the best will receive a High Distinction. This means they have received more than 75 marks out of 100. (In the 'old days' a student had to receive 85 marks out of 100 to receive a High Distinction or Honours.) How times have changed. Now some systems award a 'pass' if the student gets 40 points out of 100.

The whole experience these days is designed to be encouraging. It used to be difficult to pass an exam; it is now difficult to fail. While, in my opinion, this is not necessarily a good thing, many over-protective parents and educators disagree as they feel it is necessary to molly coddle the children.

What Are the Benefits of Sitting Exams for Dance?

1. Sitting exams means following a set syllabus, one that has been devised by a recognised organisation, either national or international.
   When I sat my Elementary Exam, aged twelve in New Zealand, it was based on two years of studying the Royal Academy of Dance Syllabus. The visiting examiner was Martin Rubenstein who was a former Principal Dancer with the Borovansky (now Australian Ballet). A highly respected and very tough examiner. We were all shaking in our ballet shoes. Out of the whole country, Mr Rubenstein awarded only four 'Honours' which was the highest mark achievable and required 85 or more points. The four 'Honours' were all from the same teacher, Lorraine Peters, and I was one of the four. Two years later the visiting examiner was from the UK. There were similar results from our teacher's students and again I was one of the students with the high marks and following that I was selected into the final six dancers in the country to try for the Royal Academy of Dance Scholarship. The prize was a full scholarship to the Royal Ballet School.
2. The student has a set timeframe to get ready to sit the exam, which encourages more focus, concentration, discipline and improvement. If there is no time limit as to when the student has to have a step corrected or a combination 'cleaned', then sometimes they never reach their best.

3. The student learns to deal with nerves and 'butterflies', which is necessary if they are going to be a performer. Students need to learn how to control their nervousness so that it works to their advantage. Many students go to pieces in an exam because the nerves get the better of them, and other students rise to the occasion. All teachers will agree that sometimes the student they expect will attain a high mark, in fact doesn't; and the student they thought deserved an average mark comes out with the top mark. There is a lot of information in books and on the internet on strategies to control mindset and nerves and these are worth looking into if the student wishes to pursue a path in the performing arts.
4. One of the top benefits of sitting exams is the sense of achievement the student feels when they pass and hold the certificate, and sometimes a medal, in their hand. Working for months to be as proficient as possible at the exam work, whatever the genre is, and going through the nerve-wracking experience of sitting the exam, then having the news that they have passed is very exciting. As well as being a learning experience, it builds self-esteem and confidence. Students get to know how they perform under pressure and realise what they need to work on in the future.
5. The majority of students enjoy participating in examinations.
6. Certificates in dance can go towards school certificates. For example, passing the Royal Academy of Dance and Australian Teachers of Dancing Vocational Exams (and many others) means a point towards the Year 12 School Certificate. These points are for the major vocational exams and not the grade exams.
7. The student's technique and overall dance standard are raised to a considerably higher standard than they would be otherwise. The work done in the lead up to exams transfers into better competition performances and standards.
8. A wonderful benefit of sitting examinations is that it can put a student well on the path to becoming a teacher later on.

CHAPTER 17

Concerts

Dance school concerts are a favourite for all dance students. For many children this is the highlight of the year. It's a chance to get onstage, to wear costumes and makeup and to have fun performing for family and friends in a theatre. It's very exciting indeed.

Teachers put an enormous amount of work into the choreography and rehearsals for these much-anticipated concerts. Parents spend a lot of time running their children to extra rehearsals. Usually, the costume cost is built into the term fees.

Putting on a dance school concert is a huge undertaking for the directors and staff and the organisation of the whole thing requires considerable stamina. Is it a sign of the times that directors and teachers nowadays receive many derogatory comments and complaints from disgruntled parents? Most parents and families have absolutely no idea of what's involved in staging a concert of this nature. No matter how good or bad the show is, the organisers should be applauded and thanked for undertaking such a massive project. The parents who appreciate their efforts and are very happy with the outcome rarely seem to voice their thanks. Complaints can range from the fact that little Johnny was in the second row of the dance and the mother thought he should be in the front, to little Susie's aunty didn't like the music or the costume. I mean seriously! Showing gratitude and appreciation would go a long way.

Earlier, we recognised the need for parents to have a voice when it comes to their children's dance training and to keep a firm eye on what's being taught and by whom. From the music the children are dancing to, to the costumes and choreography, parents must feel free to politely speak up and communicate with the teachers and studio owners. During the year and leading up to any performances and the end-of-year concert, this is a MUST. However, once the concert or performance is over, some parents may be unhappy about their child not doing a solo or not being in the front row, for instance. If they have sent their child to a high-quality teacher, then they must trust that the teacher has cast the dance in the manner they see fit. In this case it is not appropriate for the parent to question the teacher's decision in casting. There are many varied reasons for who is cast as a soloist or leader. Children must learn that not everyone can be centre stage. At the end of the day, if parents are really not happy, there are plenty of other studios to choose from.

Send a 'thank you' email to teachers and staff after the concert (or be old-fashioned and send a card) for all their efforts during the year and for putting on the concert.

Every studio has a few parents who, through fair means or foul, try to dictate to the teacher who they should put in the front of their routines. This happens in competitions too. Thankfully, most teachers have the integrity to stand up to this type of bullying from the parents, as it is never acceptable to have certain parents virtually running the studios. They manipulate the teachers by threatening to leave the studio; they spread gossip; or they just complain so often and so harshly that the teacher gives in just to shut them up. Studios are far better off without this type of parent, no matter how talented their child is.

A student who endures this sort of parental intervention will be unlikely to succeed in dance in the future.

Concerts should be entertaining and many of them are as the teachers of extremely high calibre put extensive thought into the choreography, costumes and staging. Creating a cohesive all-round show is an art in itself and it's so wonderful to witness top-class concerts such as these.

But not all concerts are entertaining. At the age of about twelve years, I went to watch my friend's dance concert and was never so bored in my life. I had ambitions to be a dance teacher even at that age and swore to myself that I would do everything I possibly could not to bore the audience at any dance concerts I put on. Hopefully, I have kept that promise to myself.

It is a case of 'the more the merrier' at concerts these days. Whereas a dance concert would be around ninety minutes long at the most, with an interval of about fifteen minutes, now the concerts can go on for hours and hours. I feel sorry for the people in the audience who are not very interested in dance but go to support a family member, and who are subjected to this—especially the brothers and dads. So many times, instead of them seeing a showcase of high calibre, they have to endure dance after dance after dance of every class in the school and the continuous procession of routines that look very similar to each other in their eyes. Instead of being entertained, they are bored to tears and loathe having to endure the yearly concert.

The problem with the length and repetitiveness of some concerts these days can be attributed to the fact that each student participates in so many routines. I have seen students who have been in up to twenty routines in one concert. It's absurd. They barely have time to change costumes before they're onstage again and we see them get more and more tired as the show goes on. It's too much—both for them and the audience! It all works much better if the students do no more than one routine per genre that they are learning and do it to the highest standard possible. In this way, the concert will a good and bearable length and the audience will be entertained, hopefully looking forward to returning the following year.

It is during the lead up to the end-of-year concert that children are at a vulnerable stage. With extra activities at school, perhaps school exams and so on, they are coming to the end of the year. With the extra rehearsals and more energy required, parents must make sure their children don't get too exhausted. Take extra care with nutrition and hydration and make sure they get enough rest and sleep. When extra pressure is put on students at this time, they can become prone to illness and injury.

CHAPTER 18

Bullying

Unfortunately, bullying seems to rear its ugly head in dance studios, usually brought about by one student's jealousy of another. The worst case I have been told about was when one student actually threatened to stab another dancer. The two had been having an ongoing feud due to jealously and even though this was reported to the directors of the studio they would not take action as they said they needed the fees from the offending student. It is unbelievable that this was the response. The threatened student left the studio that she had trained at for several years.

Other types of bullying on social media and comments made to students face to face are intolerable and totally unacceptable. I have heard students bullying others because they pulled out of the 'competition team' (because their parents couldn't afford to keep going). I've heard of a student being bullied because she could only afford to do ballet lessons and not the whole package because her mother had just been through cancer treatment. The studio bullied her and her family by telling her she had to do more classes or leave. So she left.

Students bully others because they get to do the solo in the group dance and as soon as they make a mistake, some of the others pounce on them, verbally abusing them.

I've heard of teachers bullying students into doing workshops and verbally abusing students who wish to leave the studio. It's all intolerable.

We are in a particularly difficult position when the teacher/s or studio directors are the ones doing the bullying because it is paramount that those in charge set a good example and are good role models.

Studios must have zero tolerance for bullying and a strong bullying policy. Students must be comfortable reporting any bullying to their teachers, knowing it will be dealt with satisfactorily. It is a good idea to have one or two senior students who act as prefects and can talk to the teachers and studio owners on behalf of the students. This is particularly effective if the student is reluctant to bring the bullying (or any other) issue to the attention of the staff.

CHAPTER 19

Body Image, Nutrition and Overall Care

There is a dark side to the dance culture that is often swept under the carpet. The need to 'look good' in the costumes for group performance, and the students' constant comparing of themselves to other students (largely brought on by the overuse of mirrors in studios) has encouraged body-image insecurities in young dance students, sometimes leading to eating disorders and mental illness. Many competition group costumes are not designed for a variety of shapes, sizes and figures and are often rather unforgiving for some children who may not naturally be flattered by hipster tights and a skimpy crop top, for instance.

This is not helped by the fact that professional dancers have the reputation for being slim. Care must be taken to ensure dance students don't take it upon themselves to reduce their nutrition to attain a low body weight by excessive dieting. Not all bodies are suited to professional careers, but no dance student should feel pressured by anyone, or themselves, to fit into any particular expectation regarding their body.

Many experts in the field of nutrition and eating disorders have written books, blogs, and intellectual papers. And much information can be found online.

Back in the day, many dancers would smoke cigarettes to keep their weight down or go on dangerous diets, but nowadays there is much knowledge available around this subject and many medical experts and psychologists can help the student who is in need of it.

The studio and teachers should set a positive example by never commenting to students about their own body size/type or the students'. By encouraging balanced nutrition and asking the students if they've had something nutritious during their break, for instance, the teacher is creating a positive outlook for the students. Disorders regarding eating usually start at around thirteen years of age, so full-time students and those who are ambitious for dance careers could be at risk, as well as the day students of that age.

Should the student have any problems regarding weight loss, weight gain, or any disorders, then it is up to the parents, students and doctor to implement a plan and/or solution. It's up to teachers to keep an eye open for any issues regarding any areas of concern and to voice any concerns to the parents.

Moreover, it would be beneficial for studios to engage professional specialists in nutrition, physiotherapy, psychology, time management and overall care to come and talk to the students.

In addition, care must be taken that the students are not run ragged physically, psychologically or emotionally, and it's up to parents and teachers to keep a close eye on the children. Sometimes students need to take some time out to recharge their batteries.

Children and young adults who are engaged in dance training also need to make sure their nutrition is adequate and that they get enough sleep, hydration, and rest.

CHAPTER 20

Dance Attire, Shoes, Costumes, Hair and Makeup

We have already established that care must be taken with costuming for concerts and eisteddfods/competitions, especially in the group dances. As children come in all shapes and sizes, larger students should not be made feel self-conscious by having to wear costumes that are better suited to a slim figure. For instance, a child whose physique isn't suited to a costume with a bare midriff will feel embarrassed and will lose confidence and self-esteem when, inevitably, derogatory comments come from some peers. It's not an ideal situation and not fair on the child. Tricks with costumes are many and include wearing a body stocking under any costumes that show bare skin.

Costumes don't need to be expensive to be effective. Many costumes are bought from websites that supply from overseas. Gone are the good old days when the parents (well, the mums) would have a meeting with the head mum of each concert dance, who would produce paper copies of costumes, together with the material and any sequins etc. Our mums all knew how to sew, and it was very exciting to see the costume come to life as they toiled at their sewing machines and the cat ran around the house with net stuck to it. What a moment when the costume was finally finished, and our mums would nervously take it to the dress rehearsal hoping it was right and that no-one would notice a few untidy bits on the inside. No Lycra back then and no stretch satin.

There are simple and effective ways of making costumes look good onstage without spending a fortune.

My own daughter when going to the New York finals of the Internationally renowned dance competition, the Youth America Grands Prix wore a fabulous tutu for her 'Kitri' Act 3 solo. It was not a new tutu. We used a red half-tutu skirt to which I added more layers of net. We also had a very old tutu bodice made in the traditional way with rows of hooks-and-eyes at the back. It fitted her like a glove, and I attached it to the half-tutu skirt. I then found a beautiful black silk evening gown at an op shop that had loads of intricate beading all over it and proceeded to cut it up and arrange it over the tutu. After adding black lace etc., the tutu sat beautifully and looked fantastic onstage. When she danced at the McDonalds Ballet Scholarship finals at the Sydney Opera House she had earnt her thousand-dollar tutu, which we had made from scratch by an esteemed tutu maker in Sydney.

Little children don't need elaborate costumes or tutus. Indeed, these days when we see the little ones in their expensive tutus, the costume doesn't match up with the dancing. In competitions, the costumes form part of the overall performance mark. They're marked for their appropriateness for the dance they're performing, as well as their age appropriateness and so on. But a costume that costs a thousand dollars may not be as effective as one that costs a hundred dollars.

One of the main things to remember is to make sure the student dances in the costume before they perform in it onstage. Tights should be worn with all costumes. Some eisteddfods now have that rule in their syllabus.

Make sure the costume is fastened well so it doesn't come undone onstage, ride up, or move into the wrong places. Goodness knows how many times we have seen the 'wedgie' where the costume has had a severe case of 'ride up'; or adjudicating whilst holding one's breath as the costume 'rides down'! Very embarrassing for all. Or the strap that suddenly snaps leaving the dancer to either run offstage or try to hold the costume together for the rest of the dance.

Ensure that all head pieces are clipped on properly. It's best to go overboard with bobby pins than to have the head piece fly off into the audience mid-pirouette! There is no need to wear more than one

Dance Attire, Shoes, Costumes, Hair and Makeup

head piece at a time. I have seen dancers who have worn a tiara, flowers around the bun, and a feather at the side. It's too much. Less is more.

Check and double check head piece, costume, tights, and shoes before going onstage.

Ballet shoes can be problematic. We adjudicators often see the ends of ribbons coming unstuck, which is rather distracting. Part of the discipline of dance is to make sure shoe ribbons are firmly out of sight. Children don't automatically know how to do this and must be taught. There are various methods that can be used to secure shoe ribbons but do not use Sellotape, as it catches the light and shines.

Another no-no is to let your underwear show below your costume. For example, a lovely dancer wearing a beautiful tutu ruins the illusion when the audience notices her underwear creeping down from the tutu bottom.

Sequins, crystals and other additions to costumes should be sewn and not glued on. If they fall off onto the floor it is distracting for the audience and can cause the dancer to slip over on them. Any feathers should be hair-sprayed. There are many more tricks of the trade that teachers would know about, so it's up to parents and students to ask for help if needed.

Uniforms for classes are usually made compulsory by the studio and teachers. Children love to wear a uniform. It gives them a sense of belonging to the class they are in. So it's advisable to buy the uniform and shoes ready to start the classes. A different leotard might be required for different styles of dance, so it's best to check when enrolling what the requirements are. Some schools have a 'pre-loved' shop, which is a great idea for dance uniforms and shoes as the children almost always grow out of them rather than wear them out and it can get expensive to buy new ones each year. Most schools now also have tracksuits and t-shirts etc. as additional options

If the dance shoes are getting worn and scuffed, sometimes they can be painted. As a cost-saving idea, look for a specific colour that matches the original colour.

Once the dancer progresses to pointe work, then the pointe shoes require special treatment. Firstly, the student must book into a dance boutique for a pointe-shoe fitting. It's important that the person conducting the fitting is a genuine specialist, as much money can be wasted, and damage done to feet and ankles, if given the wrong pointe shoes. Given the vast range of pointe shoes available, help is needed to find the right ones. There is information available on the internet regarding how pointe shoes should be fitted, and an experienced ballet teacher will tell you what to look for. The sewing on of ribbons and elastic is specific also, and parents should seek help from teachers regarding the right way to do this.

Pointe shoes should never be stuffed into the ballet bag and left there until the next lesson. They will break down due to the sweat and heat from the feet, especially in a humid climate. The shoes must be taken out of the bag and hung up by the ribbons to air, along with any toe pads etc.

How exciting it is to put on makeup for the stage! Most children like to dress up and makeup is part of the dressing-up fun. Stage makeup should be kept basic and simple, however, especially for young children. Even though they're onstage they should still look their age and there's no need to plaster makeup and false eyelashes on young children. Similarly, sequins and glitter should be kept off the face as they don't enhance the dancer's face onstage.

A basic foundation, blush, eyebrow pencil, eyeliner, brown eye shadow, mascara, and an appropriate lipstick are all that are needed. Green, blue or purple eyeshadow does not look well under most lighting, and at competitions sometimes the lighting is so sparse that instead of seeing the dancers' eyes we see blobs of green, blue or purple.

The idea of stage makeup is to highlight the eyes and mouth so the audience can see the expressions of the dancers better.

Hairstyles for dance differ, of course, depending on what style of dance is being performed. Part of the discipline of dance is to have the correct uniform shoes and hairstyle for your classes as well as performances. It should be insisted upon by teachers that the students are correctly attired for all of their classes, and don't turn up looking like a rabble.

This means, clean tights and shoes, correct leotard and hair done properly, no jewellery dangling down and no watches, bangles or bracelets. Students have sometimes asked why they can't wear hooped earrings to dancing lessons and the answer is because a dancer's ear can get ripped when another dancer's finger gets caught in her earring. Similarly, watches can scratch another dancer, and also break the line of your arms. It generally looks untidy. If students are looking to follow a professional career, rules are there to be followed and it's all part of the discipline of dance.

Hair should be off the face for all styles of dance. For jazz/tap, for example, hair in a ponytail; for ballet, hair should always be in a bun or similar secure style. Children do better if they are properly dressed and this discipline translates through to their dancing. A child who is untidy in appearance will often be untidy in their dancing as well.

CHAPTER 21

Code of Conduct for Parents

Parents of dance students should remain realistic—they should keep their feet on the ground and keep things in perspective. It used to be said that if a student was talented, 'for goodness sake don't tell the mother', and for good reason, as many mothers do tend to get carried away, especially nowadays with the exaggerated praise that's often given.

> Undoubtedly it is important to teach the young students a general knowledge of ballet and try to interest them in this magnificent art, but you need to do it right and understand what is possible and what is impossible! […] but in many schools around the world, where parental ambitions often take over, this process is not followed […]
>
> (Fethon Miozzi, Ballet teacher of the middle and senior classes in the Vaganova Ballet Academy of St Petersburg, Facebook)

As a parent you need to keep a close eye on what's going on in your child's dance lessons and at the studio in general. You can also help your child cope with disappointments (of which there are bound to be at least several), and injuries. Finding physiotherapists, medical practitioners, and other health professionals is part of your job too, as a support for your child.

When helping your child cope with disappointment, this shouldn't involve making excuses or blaming others. Using disappointment as an opportunity to learn and grow is a good way forward.

It is your job as a parent to make sure your child gets to the classes on time and is correctly dressed, taking with them what is required. Make sure your child's nutrition and rest is sufficient and that dance is balanced with other activities and school.

Parents Must Not Try to Run the Dance Studio

If you do your research thoroughly to begin with when finding a dance studio and teacher/s, you can then leave it up to the qualified teachers you have chosen. Once your child is in the hands of truly qualified and experienced teachers, you must back off and limit yourself to observing and encouraging. The teacher, if chosen correctly, has the expertise in dance. The parent does not!

Some parents seem to think they know more than the teacher just because they've sat in on a few lessons or learnt dancing for a couple of years when they were younger. Teaching dance is a many layered art and students are developed slowly. It takes twelve years to train a dancer. Parents mustn't want instant success or results. It's not just about pointing your toes, doing a few tricks, and smiling.

While the majority of dance parents are well-meaning, supportive, encouraging and wonderful, a few parents will continually try to tell the teacher/studio owner what to do and what not to do. Some have tried to intimidate the teacher to the point where the teacher is too scared not to put their child in the front of the routine or give them a leading role in the concert.

Teachers have a lot to deal with when parents try to wield power over them. Studio owners and directors must be careful to fully support their teachers and students and not cross the line of allowing certain parents to 'call the shots'. If a child is talented and the parent threatens to take the child to another studio if they're not given the solo in the concert, for example, then the teacher must let that child go. A studio is far better off without this type of parent. Students must be allowed to 'paddle their own canoe' and too often an overly interfering parent has not only caused trouble for the studio and the teachers but also for the student.

A growing concern in this day and age is that teachers and studio owners are much more accessible than ever before. They are accessible due to technology. They are not as accessible in person. It is always best to ask for a short meeting with a teacher or studio owner if a parent has any concerns regarding their child's dance classes. It is the responsibility of the studio owner to organise this. It is not acceptable for a parent to 'bail up' a teacher before or after a class. The teacher is not prepared, and the discussion takes away class time from other students. The teacher may be on their way home or to another job. Parents must have respect and consideration for the teachers. Similarly, the parents and students must be respected, and their grievances heard. It is not acceptable for parents to gossip about teachers or other students. It is not acceptable for teachers to gossip about other teachers or students to parents.

The code of behaviour for parents is intended to support you to reassure your child that dance is for enjoyment and that they are loved for themselves rather than for their achievements.

1. If children are interested, encourage them to dance. Do not force them.
2. Remember, children are dancing for their enjoyment, not yours.
3. Encourage dance students to see live professional performances as often as possible.
4. Don't focus on winning. Focus instead on efforts and performance rather than the overall outcome of the examination, performance, or audition.
5. Help children to set realistic goals based on their individual ability and experience.
6. Teach children that an honest effort is as important as a victory, so that the results of each examination or performance are accepted without too much disappointment.
7. Never ridicule or yell at a child for making a mistake or not passing an examination.
8. Remember that children learn best by example. Applaud good performances by all of the performers.

Code of Conduct for Parents

In the years to come your children will grow up and remember their dancing days. Dance teachers have enormous influence over youngsters' lives and carry a great responsibility.

Whether they end up dancing professionally or not, they will have learnt a lot about many things. I can still remember my first teacher telling us that if we learnt nothing else from ballet, we would know how to get out of a sports car elegantly. She was the same teacher who would tell parents that their daughter would be better off trying horse riding than ballet. No gilding the lily in those days!

However with the right teaching and guidance a dance student will gain many life skills through dance.

We want our children to have happy memories of their dancing days and many of them will still be friends with their dancing buddies long after they've hung up their shoes. Personally, I am still in touch with many of my 'old' students—some of whom have told me that their dancing days were the best days of their lives.

We don't want our children to be suffering physical pain from the injuries they've sustained or have memories of being driven so hard that they grew to hate dancing. Let the children enjoy their dance journey through a happy, honest and safe dance education.

CHAPTER 22

What Dance Professionals Say

Nicole Ashfield – Dip ABS, LATOD, ARAD

Nicole Ashfield was originally trained by her mother, Avril Binzer, and then later with Paul Hammond in Melbourne. She successfully auditioned for The Australian Ballet School in 1967 and graduated in 1969. At the ballet school, she trained under such luminaries as Dame Margaret Scott, Dame Peggy Van Praagh and Leon Kellaway, to name a few.

Her dance career has been diverse including dancing in musicals, operas, winning the World Amateur Latin American championship in 1967 and being involved in the production of Nureyev's version of *Don Quixote* in 1970.

She then began teaching in partnership with her mother at the Binzer Schools of Ballet and Modern Dance in Glen Waverley, Melbourne, until moving to Queensland with her family in 1977. In 1979, Nicole opened her own school, Ashfield Ballet School, in Cleveland, which quickly grew into one of the largest and most successful ballet schools in the Redlands area of Brisbane. Her school, now in its fortieth year, boasts a wonderful faculty of teachers, including her two daughters.

Nicole's school has a permanent studio in Capalaba in addition to its six other branches around the Redlands City area. Nicole has been an Examiner for ATOD (Australian Teachers of Dancing) since its inception in 1991 and was made a Life Member in 2006. She was also invited to be a Life Member of the Royal Academy of Dance in 2007.

In 2006, she was awarded the Avril Binzer Memorial Award for her service and dedication to ATOD. She has also been an integral member of the core committee for the new Classical Ballet Syllabus as well as the National Character Syllabus.

###

I commented to Nicole that it must be difficult for parents to find genuinely top-quality dance lessons these days because there is such a lot of 'spin' put on social media and online advertisements. I asked her what she saw as the biggest challenge for dance parents nowadays, and what she saw as the five things a parent should look for in a dance studio or teacher.

> Finding genuine qualified teachers is the biggest challenge.
>
> Qualifications, longevity of the studio, evident love of dance and dance teaching, good communication with parents, a studio that is involved with a recognised association delivering examinations, competitions, master classes etc. that benefit their students – these are the five things a parent should look for.

What do you think are the biggest challenges for dance students?

> Fitting in their dance classes with their busy lives, working to the best of their ability, being happy with their achievements, and not comparing themselves with others.

In your experience and from your observations, what has been the biggest challenge as a studio owner and dance teacher (apart from the COVID-19 repercussions)?

> No ethics from other studios (either good or bad) starting in your area/suburb.

It has been written about all over the world – this 'flexibility freakshow' that's going on and has caused an ongoing rise of injuries (some permanent) in young dancers. What can be done to help to stop this damage? Many unqualified people are teaching this extreme stretching. Training in safe stretching and safe dance practice should be mandatory, but how can we implement this, since there is no governing body (apart from the Royal Academy of Dance, the Australian Teachers of Dancing and the British Ballet Organisation)?

> Keep talking and communicating with parents and students to explain the problems and long-term/injuries that may occur.

There are many studios offering full-time training. How can students differentiate between the courses to find out which ones are of the highest quality?

> Arrange a time to visit, take classes and meet the owners and teachers and continue to research the studios that may interest you for full-time training.

In today's dance landscape, what are the jobs that you would be steering your students towards, given that there are few professional jobs available? Ballet companies in Russia are even cutting their dancers by 20 per cent at the moment. Is aiming for a professional career still viable?

> Dancers should be versatile and prepared to adapt to new circumstances. Very few students have full classical ballet ability and should not be training only in classical ballet. Students should be very open-minded and have thought of other career options.

Various teachers and studio owners don't seem to have a good grip on the professional world of dance. It has been brought to my attention over the years that a fair bit of unrealistic advice has been dished out to students, which has misled them into believing they are far more talented that what they actually are and made them falsely believe they have potential for professional careers. Where can students go to get impartial advice and an honest appraisal of their talent and potential? Do you think they should get a second or third opinion before embarking on full-time training?

> In reality, yes, but families are brainwashed into thinking their studio is amazing and so continue to pay exorbitant fees for full-time training. Once again they need to research full-time training facilities and find out if their students are given opportunities to follow on with their dance careers in other ways than just performing.

How can highly trained/experienced teachers win the 'tug-of-war' between proper teaching and the fact that parents and students are lured into going to 'bad' teachers because they teach tricks and extreme movements/stretching that they see on social media and shows like *Dance Moms*?

> This tug-of-war may never be won but the 'good' teachers continue to teach correctly, stick to their quality and integrity and hope it eventually filters through the community.

Do you think a book such as this one will help to get the message out to parents? Over the past fifteen years or so, the 'good' teachers I have spoken to around Australia and New Zealand are all in agreement that the message and information need to somehow reach parents to help stop the extreme training that's damaging children worldwide. There has been much written in the media about this problem, along with the 'sexualisation of young dancers' with age-inappropriate costumes, choreography and music.

> Yes, books like this should help to get the message out there.

Do you agree that the adjudicators that reward extreme movements and age-inappropriate performances should stop and instead reward quality of movement, good technique, artistry etc.?

> We have said this for many years, but many adjudicators continue to say one thing and do another.

Are there any other methods that you see as being useful in educating the public and steering parents and children towards finding genuine top-quality schools?

> Not really as this is the 'arts' and there will always be differing opinions.

Do you agree that talented children should be taken out of school and put into performing arts programs where they 'home-school' at the studio and dance every afternoon, and all day on Saturdays?

> No!

If they are put into these schools at an early age, is it fair to say that their bodies could develop unsuitably for dancing or their interest in dance may change as they might want to pursue a different career?

> Yes!

At what age should a student go into full-time training? Should they finish high school first, so they have a well-rounded education?

> Yes they should finish high school and take on full-time training when they are old enough to then follow on with a career. If they are wanting to leave earlier to train for a longer period, they should still finish their education but be at least Grade 10 and be warned about burnout and overtraining.

I have seen evidence of young children's parents being coerced into sending their children to daytime and full-time training at an early age who are not actually talented. It breaks my heart. What are your thoughts on this type of solicitation? Is there anything that can be done to stop this sort of thing going on?

> Yes I have also seen this, but unfortunately some teachers/studios are in it for the money and will do all they can to convince parents it is the right thing to do. I believe it is wrong as younger students need to be at school in a normal environment growing up with extracurricular activities open to them.

The dance industry is one of the only activities involving a large number of children that is not regulated. Over the years some have tried unsuccessfully to find a way to regulate the industry. This is a big problem as anyone can set up a dance studio and teach dance. (Some claim obscure qualifications and experience, pulling the wool over parents' eyes.) In light of this, how can parents be safeguarded against bad dance teaching practices? Do you think there will ever be a way that dance may be regulated in the future?

> If qualifications had to be all advertised, this would help but this not going to happen with the extended dance community of hip-hop etc.

Generally, do you think enough attention is paid to proper technique in junior students, or is there too much focus on tricks, flexibility?

> Technique can be boring to young students and 'tricks' are fun! A good teacher can overcome this and retain their students who will then have a chance of learning correctly.

Do you think students learn too many styles too early and never achieve a solid technique in anything in particular?

> There is so much more now than years ago. In so many cases, yes this happens.

Is ballet still the necessary and best genre to learn to give a solid base for other genres?

> A solid classical ballet basic training is the only way students can go on to other genres.

Many studios sell package deals to children from a young age, which include several dance styles. How many classes/styles should children be doing, between ages five and twelve?

It depends on the child, but ballet, jazz and tap are a good start.

How important is it for children to have a balance in their lives and not to be at the dance studio every day after school for hours on end and most weekends?

Balance is important, but if they love their dancing it can work as it does with sport.

Have competitions gotten out of control? Most studios these days seem to advertise the success of their students at competitions as a form of free advertising. Is there too much emphasis on competition success these days?

Children do love performing and this should be the emphasis – not the competing.

When adjudicating I don't often see good, solid technique and there is a lack of actual 'steps' in ballet and combinations in jazz. Many contemporary solos seem to be churned out to a formula. Lyrical solos are often sloppy and overall there is a lack of musicality. Do teachers have too many students in competitions and not enough time to put thought into the dances? Do you think students are doing too many solos—'Jack/Jill' of all trades?

We do, but most teachers do not choreograph their own routines (groups or solos) so much choreography is just repeated for a different child or group by a so-called choreographer who is in it for the money and charges heaps for teaching the same or similar routine over and over to different studios/students. Not a lot of thought goes into the ability of the student or the coordination and connection of the music and steps.

Nicole, you have had to adapt and cater to many changes over the past forty years that your school has been operating. What has been the most difficult and challenging adaptation you have had to make?

> Taking on the different genres to cater for students who would go elsewhere if we did not offer the range of genres. This COVID-19 time has never been faced before by any studio even when my mum [Averil Binzer] was teaching in the 1940s through World War Two. Many studios are still not social distancing or following the COVID-19 rules.

How important is it to learn a nationally or internationally recognised syllabus?

> I believe it is very important to belong to a recognised dance association.

How important are exams?

> We place a lot of importance on examinations as it gives students a sense of achievement and our students love doing them.

Do parents have too much to say these days or do you welcome their input? Some studios seem to allow parents to run them, dictating who does solos etc., and threatening to leave the studio if they don't get their own way, for example.

> We keep our parents away from the running of the studio and decision-making for solos etc. If they are unhappy with our decisions they are better off leaving and not influencing other families. Yes, some studios let this happen too much and it causes a lot of trouble.

Paul Malek

Paul Malek is one of the most highly regarded directors and choreographers in Australia. With a passion for education, self-empowerment and artistic innovation, he inspires many individuals, businesses and communities to strive towards becoming the greatest version of themselves possible whilst nurturing artistic development and professional growth.

Trained in Classical Ballet and Contemporary Dance at the Victorian College of the Arts Secondary School, his performing career saw him tour the world through all five continents as dancer, dance captain, rehearsal director and company manager, all before the age of 25.

Returning to Australia in 2006, he became an avid entrepreneur, creating businesses such as Collaboration the Project (2008–2014), responsible for events such as UNDRGRND Melbourne, Sydney and Brisbane, Immersed Melbourne Dance Industry Night, DANCE CHAT and DANCE CHAT LIVE, Project Y (youth dance company) and over 16 professional production seasons and tours. Paul Malek is the original Founder and Director of popular Melbourne Dance Institute MAPA Australia (2006–2011), and was also the co-director of BOOM Media, a Marketing and Media Company, For Dancers by Dancers from 2011 to 2015.

Currently a choreographic regular on *Dancing with the Stars* and *So You Think You Can Dance Australia* (seasons 3 & 4), Paul has been the choreographic brains of well over a hundred corporate events, award ceremonies, television commercials, music videos and dance festivals over the last decade.

In 2015, Malek founded Transit Dance, and currently resides as Artistic Director overseeing the immense output of performance platforms and educational opportunities created from within their state-of-the-art dance and performance precinct in Brunswick, Victoria.

During his day-to-day commitments at Transit Dance, he is also a highly sought-after host and inspirational speaker, speaking at many corporate events, conventions and festivals not only in Australia but across the globe.

###

I put it to Paul that it must be difficult for parents to find genuinely top-quality dance lessons these days as there is such a lot of 'spin' put on social media and online advertisements. What do you see is the biggest challenge for dance parents nowadays?

What Dance Professionals Say

> The parents' challenge begins with finding a place that will not only be a safe and holistic learning environment, but also a place that gives their child true happiness in their learning. This comes up against a few simple hurdles. Friendship groups, popularity and the requirement to belong become key factors in the decision-making of young students, especially when moving into their adolescence. This can create a displacement of opinion of what is right, safe and beneficial to what is wanted. What we want can confuse decisions about what is best, and what is best is very rarely the school touting they are the best. For being the best requires much more than your ability physically; it involves mentality, approach, respect and diligence. Hence why a holistic approach to dance learning at a young age is integral when searching for a school.

What are the five things a parent should look for in a dance studio/teacher?

> Transparency, kindness, respect, knowledge and the ability to communicate this knowledge with great care and passion.

What do you think are the biggest challenges for dance students?

> Understanding that they are enough, worthy and capable of achieving great things in their life. No matter what the person standing next to them or in front of them is doing, they are on their own journey and that in itself is a beautiful thing.

In your experience and from your observations, what has been the biggest challenge as a studio owner and dance teacher (apart from the COVID-19 repercussions)?

> Patience. I think it applies to many different areas in our lives. The need to apply it personally to your business, to your clients, to your students, to their families, to your staff. Mastering patience is a challenge when life gets busy and your passion to say yes and please everyone takes flight. Learning

to say no, learning to hit pause, learning to act, not react and, above all else, demonstrate patience when creating and delivering your passion.

It has been written about all over the world—this 'flexibility freakshow' that's going on and has caused an ongoing rise of injuries (some permanent) in young dancers. What can be done to help to stop this damage? Many unqualified people are teaching this extreme stretching. Training in safe stretching and safe dance practice should be mandatory, but how can we implement this, since there is no governing body (apart from the Royal Academy of Dance, the Australian Teachers of Dancing and the British Ballet Organisation)?

> It is a slippery slope that will never be solved through online debate. Without a governing body, it is almost impossible, and with a governing body will they ever truly have the power to police bad practice?
>
> Qualifications and professional development should be mandatory in this day and age, and with so many professional development opportunities online, there should be a great push towards an evolution of dance education for the safety of the young human beings under teachers' care.

In today's dance landscape, what are the jobs that you would be steering your students towards, given that there are few professional jobs available? Ballet companies in Russia are even cutting their dancers by 20 per cent at the moment. Is aiming for a professional career still viable?

> Dance in itself is a growing industry. Cruise-ship employment is at an all-time high. Contemporary dance through Europe is a well-supported, attended art-form. The dance teaching industry is expanding greatly. Independent companies are increasing and not to mention major musicals, Cirque productions and big-budget movies adding to the scope of performing arts. There is actually a great world out there with many opportunities. It is

just navigating and educating further on the how to get there, instead of focusing on the what. (Of course, I am not heading down the COVID road with this response!)

Do you think a book such as this one will help to get the message out to parents? Over the past fifteen years or so, the 'good' teachers I have spoken to around Australia and New Zealand are all in agreement that the message and information needs to somehow reach parents to help stop the extreme training that's damaging children worldwide. There has been much written in the media about this problem along with the 'sexualisation of young dancers' with age-inappropriate costumes, choreography and music.

> The more that is published around such issues in dance the better. There seems to be a stigma that as soon as something is written, observed or analysed that could negatively impact a business or a person's practice, then the gloves come off and the defence begins. It can turn ugly and on multiple occasions in my career there have been smear campaigns to discredit me just because I have spoken out or written an article regarding such concerns. There is great pride in the dance teaching industry, and that in itself can be something beautiful. However, when pride overcomes fact and the defence of one's teachings takes first priority over what is right, there is the concern. Great educators never stop learning, and great educators can also admit they were once wrong to become right.

Are there any other methods that you see as being useful in educating the public and steering parents and children towards finding genuine top-quality schools?

> The most important thing to be a quality school is to uphold quality and integrity in everything you do. That includes marketing and communication. To get your message out there is just as important as teaching your message within the studio walls.

Do you agree that talented children should be taken out of school and put into performing arts programs where they 'home-school' at the studio and dance every afternoon, and all day on Saturdays?

> If you are a full-time dancer, including if you are studying full-time professional dance, coupled with your academic studies, my main point would be weekends are off. Adolescent students need to live, learn and grow in society as well as in a studio. Downtime, the ability to work, earn money and socialise with friends is just as important as the lessons they receive in the studio.

If they are put into these schools at an early age, is it fair to say that their bodies could develop unsuitably for dancing or their interest in dance may change as they might want to pursue a different career?

> It is very much the case, that is why the program they are put into should be a holistic program that focuses evenly on their academic studies as well as their dance subjects.

At what age should a student go into full-time training? Should they finish high school first, so they have a well-rounded education?

> If they are not part of a performing arts academy/high school, then they most definitely should finish high school before attending a full-time institution. There are professional institutes that cater for professional-level training that offer and supply the ability to finish their high school education as part of their course. Every person is case by case, but in my experience as a director of a full-time institution and now academy, those who are older going into full-time training get the most out of it due to the maturity they bring to their training.

The dance industry is one of the only activities involving a large number of children that is not regulated. Over the years some have tried unsuccessfully to find a way to regulate the industry. This is a big problem as anyone can set up a dance studio and teach dance. (Some claim obscure qualifications and experience, pulling the wool over parents' eyes.) In light of this, how can parents be safeguarded against bad dance teaching practices? Do you think there will ever be a way that dance may be regulated in the future?

> I agree on so many levels to this. There need to be industry standards that need to be approved so you can advertise saying you meet these industry standards. Regulation is not something to be feared; it is something to be embraced, and the more who embrace it, the quicker we will ensure this will happen.

Generally, do you think enough attention is paid to proper technique in junior students, or is there too much focus on tricks, flexibility?

> The expression 'one trick wonder' comes to mind. It is simple, we are good at what we focus on. If we focus on a certain skill, we will be great (hopefully) at that one skill. Then we need to learn to dance. A skill is a minute portion of what it means to be a dancer. To express yourself through dance and movement is a far greater ocean than one skill, no matter how beautiful that skill can be executed. There is always so much we can be developing, exploring and achieving in dance.

Do you think students learn too many styles too early and never achieve a solid technique in anything in particular?

> I've said this saying once before, is it better to become the master of one, or become mediocre at everything. It's a tricky one, as I know that I studied all styles as a youngster, then I moved into a classical and contemporary focused program through my high school education. Then, with all the skills and artistry that came out of those six years I was able to have the skill and artistic foundation to go and do whatever I wished. Every student is different, every human is greatly different. I am

a big believer in the more we know the greater we become. But it comes down to the individual, the community they are in, and the teachers who impart dance to them.

Is ballet still the necessary and best genre to learn to give a solid base for other genres?

> Every genre has a place to give skill. Classical ballet being such a formed and consistently practised technique has great benefits as a genre to underpin many techniques in dance.

Many studios sell package deals to children from a young age, which include several dance styles. How many classes/styles should children be doing, between ages five and twelve?

> A good question, again, every dancer and child are different; however, I would say my head would explode if I was doing more than five. What would I have done, ballet, jazz, tap, drama, singing? Contemporary Dance wasn't practised at recreational/competition level when I was growing up. Although if I was growing up now, would I want more? I also played tennis, so I guess I'm not sure.

How important is it for children to have a balance in their lives and not to be at the dance studio every day after school for hours on end and most weekends?

> Balance is for all human beings. Finding balance is a constant mission. I see so many dancers live in a studio, get to their late teens and say, well now I think I am done. Which is such a shame if they were once passionate about a career in dance. A career that could take them all over the world. To do what you love every single day is an amazing thing; imagine doing that for the rest of your life. If you put it all into your youth, you may have nothing left to give when the time comes when you need to show up and make a career out of it.

What Dance Professionals Say

How important is it to learn a nationally or internationally recognised syllabus?

> I can tell you one thing; I know when someone comes into one of my courses and has been trained by a syllabus. They are clean, they have great technique, and they are well versed across multiple skills. To have a curriculum like a syllabus that is well developed and delivers creates strong dancers.

How important are exams?

> Same as my comments above. An exam is an exercise in performance, and performance is a skill we need to learn to succeed in any professional industry.

Do parents have too much to say these days or do you welcome their input? Some studios seem to allow parents to run them, dictating who does solos etc. and threatening to leave the studio if they don't get their own way, for example.

> I always appreciate feedback; it is important as a community to have it. However, feedback and commentary for improvement is very different to an upset parent causing waves due to their opinion their child is hard done by (even when they seemingly have one of the highest abilities in the class). That can be truly toxic and not necessary for your organisation and community to thrive. I like to open conversation immediately with the direct party and come to a resolution asap. If a resolution cannot be made, perhaps they aren't the right fit for your studio.

Gina-Marie Leathem ARAD Solo Seal

Gina holds the ARAD Solo Seal (Royal Academy of Dance) and has been a Professional Ballet Dancer in Europe at the Dresden Semperoper in Germany, and under the direction of Johan Kobborg at the Romanian National Ballet. She was also an apprentice at Royal NZ Ballet, under the direction of Ethan Steifel. Gina was accepted into the Vaganova Academy of Classical Ballet in St Petersburg, Russia and the Washington Ballet School in the USA. She trained at the Australian Ballet School and the prestigious Jacqueline Kennedy Onassis School at American Ballet Theatre, New York, Pre-Professional Division.

After being invited to the ABT New York Summer Intensive, Gina was named a National Training Scholar at ABT for four years. She was a finalist in the McDonalds Ballet Scholarship, Sydney; a finalist in the New York Youth America Grands Prix; and a semi-finalist at the Genée International Ballet Competition at the Royal Academy of Dance, London.

Gina has had the privilege of working with some of the very best teachers, choreographers and directors in the world. She has rubbed shoulders with dance royalty and has been in a position to observe performances by top companies and dancers in Australia, the USA, the UK and Europe. She is the recipient of many dance awards, scholarships and accolades, and is now Director of Gina-Marie Leathem Elite Ballet Coaching, Gold Coast, Australia.

###

I asked Gina about the worldwide extreme stretching craze that is dominating the junior dance world. She commented that parents need to be provided with information about how dangerous this craze is and must not support it.

> It is very dangerous as it weakens the ligaments and makes the dancer injury-prone. A professional dance partner would have great difficulty keeping a dancer on balance if they're hyperflexible, with weak ligaments.
>
> The future of young bodies is ruined, and it also prevents them from doing other sports and hobbies … Strengthening exercises are much more important than stretching. Overstretching and

extreme stretching has no useful purpose and can increase their chance of injury – potentially ending their careers.

When asked about the quest to become 'Insta-famous' by posting over-split leg mounts, tilts, needles and so on, Gina said:

I do not understand this pointless and damaging craze that, together with stretching apparatus like foot stretchers and stretching ladders, just weakens the ligaments in dance students. You should never manipulate your body by using force.'

She commented in relation to the trend in dance students learning many styles of dance that:

Too many dance styles work against each other and if the child is learning dancing as a hobby it's unnecessary to do so many styles.

Gina maintains that there must be a balance in the children's lives and parents should avoid being talked into taking 'package deals' that some big studios offer.

I asked Gina for her opinion on overtraining and full-time training. She responded:

Overtraining can lead to injuries and burnout from overuse which, for a student is unnecessary and avoidable. The children who are drawn into the world of full-time training too early can find themselves lost if a dance career doesn't work out for them. Some full-time schools do have a good balance and are age-appropriate. It's a matter of finding the right school where the studio directors care more about the wellbeing of the students than the business side.

With considerable experience at local, national and international competitions, Gina explained how important they are in developing stagecraft.

Knowing how to perform, use the wings and stage, how to do your hair, makeup and deal with being nervous are all benefits of doing competitions. However, sometimes too much importance can be put on winning, and when parents get carried away with competitions it can put a lot of pressure on the child. Not all talented dancers are 'show ponies' and some students who have extensive potential can be overlooked at competitions but have what it takes to be chosen to be trained in prestigious vocational institutions for future careers.

With regards to teams in competitions, Gina said these are usually pushed to do well as the studio's name is a stake and these are a popular way of attracting more students to the studios.

Major competitions such as YAGP and Prix de Lausanne are important for exposure and the students can be handed scholarships, apprenticeships, or even jobs at these types of competitions.

CHAPTER 23

Conclusion

The steady deterioration in standards and ethics in dance training in recent years, together with a growing lack of truth, honesty, integrity and care for dance students and parents, has led me to write this book. In using my many years of experience in professional dancing, teaching and adjudicating, as well as the experience of colleagues and experts, I hope to contribute to educating and raising parents' and children's awareness of what they are entitled to expect from a dance education.

My 'take-home' messages to parents are these. The dance industry is not regulated—anyone can open a dance studio and teach dancing and there is no consumer watchdog for dance. This means that it is very much up to you as a parent to ensure that your child is taught by someone who knows what they are doing and will not harm your child.

The sickening worldwide epidemic of dangerous stretching methods, together with the global and degrading sexualisation of young dance students, must stop. (Pseudo) teachers and parents must stop encouraging this abuse and exploitation.

Even with the best education, not every child will become a professional dancer; however, every child should be able to gain much enjoyment from dance, as well as many useful life skills and a lifelong interest.

Dancers, no matter how talented and enthusiastic, should never lose sight of their broader education. Professional dancers, and those who aspire to be professional dancers, should always have a Plan B, as dancing careers are exceedingly difficult to get and are often short-lived.

The Plan B, or parallel career, may be dance-related or not, but there must be a Plan B.

Parents must know their child. This means not pushing your child to do dance just because you want them to. As well as researching the best dance studio for your child, you must take an interest in your child's learning—but not to the point of obsession. You need to trust the teacher and the teacher must not let themselves be brow-beaten by pushy parents. At the same time, teachers and studios must respect parents, keeping them informed and not treating them like a money-pit. Parents need to have the courage to say 'no' to teachers, studios and their own children.

Above all, teachers and parents must respect the children in their care—and that includes protecting them from fads and fashions that will do them more harm than good.

You may think your child is already receiving the best, and the safest, dance training—but, armed with the knowledge provided in this book, you may need to think again. I have pulled back the curtain and shone the spotlight on the perils and pitfalls of today's dance tuition. For the sake of your children I implore you to 'look before you leap'.

For more information

Useful Websites

- Ausdance https://ausdance.org.au/
- The Ballet Blog https://www.theballetblog.com/
- Dance Success https://www.dancesuccess.org/
- International Association for Dance Medicine and Science (IADMS) https://www.iadms.org/
- Lisa Howell's Perfect Form Physiotherapy https://www.perfectformphysio.com.au/
- Safe in Dance http://www.safeindance.com/

Recognised Dance Syllabus Organisations

- Look for these when enrolling in a dance studio. Search on the internet as some offer just one style and others offer syllabi in many dance styles. (Please note this is not a complete list.) Further dance syllabi are available in various countries. *** symbolises organisations that are worldwide.
- Acrobatic Arts www.acrobaticarts.com
- Acrobatics Dance Association https://acrobaticdanceassociation.com.au/
- Australian Dance Association www.adatheatre.com.au
- Australian Dance Institute www.australiandanceinstitute.com.au
- Australian Institute of Classical Dance www.ballet.org.au
- Australian Teachers of Dancing www.atod.net.au
- Ballet Australasia Limited www.dancebal.com
- Ballet Conservatoire www.acbaustralia.com.au

- BBOdance – British Ballet Organisation www.bbodance.com ***
- British Dancing Association www.bdadance.com.au
- Cecchetti Ballet Australia www.cecchettiballet.org ***
- Classical Dance Australia (CDA)
- Comdance (formerly CSTD) www.comdance.org
- Education in Dance Theatre Arts Inc www.edta.org.au
- Les Griffith Tap Dance Academy (LGTDA)
- Movement and Dance Education Centre
- Royal Academy of Dance www.royalacademyofdance.org ***
- Southern Federation of Dance
- Tapatak Oz www.taptak.oz.com
- Wood Tap Glenn www.glennwoodtap.com

Resources Available at https://www.dancesuccess.org

Purchase your pre-competition dance routine Critique Assessments. ebooks:

- 7 Steps to Success in Dance Competitions
- How to Find the Best Dance Class for Your Child

About the Author

Dianne Leathem ARAD ATOD ADA
Member Australian Dance Adjudicators Assn
Associate Member Royal Academy of Dance
Affiliate Member Australian Teachers of Dancing
Member IADMS International Association of Dance Medicine and Science

Dianne's lifelong love of dance began aged 4½ in Christchurch, New Zealand, when she fell in love with everything about it, particularly the music. At the age of 7, inspired by seeing her first musical, *Westside Story*, she choreographed and played the lead role in her school's production of *Peter Pan*.

Dianne considers herself to be immensely fortunate to have worked with such highly esteemed, inspiring mentors as Russell Kerr QSM, ONZM, Loraine Peters QSM, Gillian Francis, Julia Barry, and Robert Young, as well as many visiting master teachers. But her gratitude extends most significantly to David Peake, formerly of the Royal Ballet, Sadlers Wells Ballet and Kiel Opera Ballet in Germany, and the Royal NZ Ballet. David's first production of *Coppelia* was an outstanding inspiration to Dianne, who greatly admired his artistry and professionalism. Under David's inspiring mentorship, she went on to partner him in major ballet productions and tours with Southern Ballet Theatre under the directorship of Russell Kerr.

Teaching most styles and specialising in Classical Ballet for over 35 years, Dianne was Director of her own large and very successful studio in New Zealand. In Australia, she was honoured to work closely with the former Patron and Life Member of ATOD, Averil Binzer, teaching and co-directing Bellder Ballet Theatre. After directing her own studio, she went on to freelance, including teaching for the renowned Prudence Bowen. She has adjudicated numerous eisteddfods and scholarships in Australia and New Zealand over many years, as well as choreographed and staged many ballets, musicals, trade shows, solos, duos, and groups for international, national, state and local competitions.

As a performer, Dianne has danced lead and solo roles in many well-known ballets, musicals, trade shows, cabaret, theatre and commercial dance and has worked extensively in television. Many of her former students have gone on to careers in ballet companies, contemporary dance, musical theatre, commercial dance, cruise ships, Disney, Universal Studios, Moulin Rouge, Lido, teaching, choreography and dance-related fields.

With a reputation for upholding the very highest standards and integrity in dance teaching and adjudicating, which were passed onto her by her esteemed teachers, Dianne has travelled extensively to observe and further her knowledge of dance and has been a guest of the Vaganova Academy of Classical Ballet in St Petersburg Russia, the American Ballet Theatre (JKO) NYC, and The Australian Ballet, and has observed in Germany, Prague, London, the Royal Academy of Dance's Genée Competition and West End Musicals, the Youth America Grands Prix NYC and numerous shows on Broadway, New York.

Dianne greatly enjoys witnessing the next generation of talent. Her increasing, heartfelt and genuine concern for the wellbeing and welfare of dance students and parents has compelled her to write *Look Before You Leap*.

www.ingramcontent.com/pod-product-compliance
Lightning Source LLC
Chambersburg PA
CBHW042139160426
43201CB00021B/2345